## Introduction

I found myself lying in bed several hours before dawn reviewing my life. Those quiet moments define the old expression, "It's darkest before the dawn". Still in a semi-sleep's hallucinogenic state, I conjured up from deep within my caverns of repressed feelings, events I could not fully engage when awake. There, I lay in my quandary, waiting for the next big issue to envelop me. Looking over my life, it seems of little consequence as to where I begin this story, as life enveloped me at its will and not of mine.

When you're six years old...

The world blasts forth like a second birth. You have little to compare new circumstances to your experience. It was an early fall morning, when times were much less tenuous and less demanding, that complexity hit me first. I remember that day, a day that has been lost in completeness but retained as a compact event with obscure details factored out. Life is trouble, no matter how you try to spin your situation. Like a spin washer flinging its debris out of the way into the path of an unsuspecting passerby. We rationalize that we are in control making sense of it all, a notion best tempered by Robert Burns, the great Scottish poet. "The best laid plans of mice and men are subject to adjustment". I have seen icons fall. I have compared myself to the great ones when convenient. When trouble touched them, it somehow made my circumstances much better. I was stunned by the death of race driver, Dale Earnhart. His life was full of the stuff we all dream of achieving. So was the daring air adventure of Steve Fossett, who flew around the world in a hot air balloon... how about Steve Irwin, the great naturalist, killed by a StingRay. The very things in which they were most accomplished led to their demise. Perhaps those of us who never reach the top of our potential are indeed fortunate. To this day, I still contemplate one great grand breakaway, an exercise in daring, carried out without fear of any impending consequence.

Flying lesions began at seventeen...

I had honed my driving skills in my 1933 Chevy. We were joined at the waist. I was ready for any new self-indulgent transportation thrill. My dad was repairing a radio set in the basement when I asked him about airplanes and flying. He didn't respond with an intelligible sound but went about his intense examination of the radio. I threw the question out for a second time, then, in a hand-on-hip stare, he said, "It isn't safe. Everyone who ever flew eventually died." The issue came up again after I learned from Phil, a saxophone player in my teenage band, that flying lessons were only $10. Phil and I had been searching for some excitement ever since my 16th birthday party. I had been driving my Chevy for about a year and figured myself as an expert on any relevant subject even remotely similar. Now this flying proposal of Phil's began to interest me. Phil pushed the issue about saving his money to buy an airplane—a fantasy by any stretch of the imagination. Phil had been looking to earn enough money just to buy an old car of his own. He didn't like to be seen in his father's old Pontiac.

My mother and dad had a deep negative opinion of Phil. He would come to my house and fill the conversation with outlandish exaggerations. "He's a
Spend-thrift," as my mother described him. "If he saved a few dollars, he would
get impatient and spend it on junk—never accumulating enough money to
get anything worthwhile, just like his father." You can see that any scheme devised by Phil would not fly at my house. The parental lectures about life were stepped up in frequency and intensity every time Phil would join band practice at my house.

My little band, the Raindrops, performed at the YMCA, the city-project jobs and teen dances—anywhere we could earn a few dollars for three hours.

In 1951, a local flying veterans group formed a drinking and dancing club.

These guys were home from the Second World War.   They were daring men, having flown over enemy territory, engaged in air combat and survived near death on a daily basis. Fear of death had been erased from their minds.

They were engaged in all sorts of dangerous activities with motorcycles, race cars and small airplanes. Through a connection with my dad, they hired my band to play every weekend at their club. We pretended to be Guy Lombardo, the present-day equivalent to the Rolling Stones. Phil got close to one of the pilots, Leader, who also worked at the local airport. Tipton Airport was anything but a classy place, grass runways with bumps and dust in the dry season and generally muddy year round. The hangar was derelict, missing windows, broken door… it resembled a toothless hillbilly hotel with petrol tanks poised outside like moonshine jugs to gravity-feed a brood of moth like creatures. Some with double wings, some with high wings, and some like miniature fighter planes. Tipton's runway was geographically placed between the prevailing winds and the

local mountains. Every pilot using this port experienced white-knuckle,

crosswind landings and tricky takeoffs on a regular basis.

Phil's new friend, Leader, invited us down to get a flying lesson a few weeks
later. It was a Sunday morning. Leader was also the life of the party at the
local air force club on Saturday night. There is an old saying about pilots:
"There are old pilots and bold pilots, but no old, bold pilots." I didn't realize
the significance of that until Sunday morning. Leader smelled like the bar
sink at the club. I was chosen to be first to get the flying lesson. It was also
my first chance to even touch an airplane. Leader figured me to be first since
I was the bandleader and commanded some respect, a lingering figment based
upon his military training.  I had never flown before. I had zero knowledge
about how these things worked.  Leader avoided ground school and simply
said, "Jump in." We sat side by side in a very small airplane; I believe he
called it, Chief.  It smacked me how much everything had a familiar look, I remembered
riding in my father's Model A Ford.  Everything looked remarkably like that old car that didn't fly.
The focus of my attention was the fuel gauge. Like the Model A's, it sat directly in front of us
outside the front window
between my feet and a strange-looking engine. I started shivering, it
was briskly cold that morning and the wind was blowing through the side

windows. Leader was smoking a cigarette and talking to one of the big
wheels of the airport. He dashed his butt to the ground and jumped into
the right side of the cockpit. I had noticed that the wings were on the top
of this little airplane and it seemed the ground would be easy to touch if
you stretched your arm out of the window. I was quickly told to hold on
to the stick (wheel-like projection) between my legs and put my feet on
the pedals.

Leader must have forgotten something as he told me, "Hold on for a second,"
and he got out and ran over to the big hangar. I continued to look over the
cockpit.  I wiggled the stick and pushed the pedals. It reminded me of the
pedal car I had used in my grandmother's backyard. I put my hand out of
the side window and felt the side door next to me. It felt thin and vulnerable
like the skin from an Indian drum. Hmm, I thought, very thin . . . actually
fragile. Leader came back to the plane and asked me if I had $5.  I did, and I
handed it over.  He went back over to the hangar and again came back with
a cigarette hanging from his lips. A new character came out of the hangar

and opened a flap on the engine.  He brought along a bottle of oil, which
looked like a mason jar with a long metal spout. He carefully tried to pour
the oil into the open hole, but most of the oil ran down over the side of the
engine. His hands seemed to shake uncontrollably.  I chalked it up to the
chilly morning air along with the after effects of the mechanic's nightlife.

I had been sitting in the plane for about fifteen minutes when Leader
stuck his last cigarette on the ground. "Ready? Here we go." Leader closed
his paper-thin side door, put a seat belt over his lap, and told me to pick my
belt up so it wouldn't get mixed up with the controls. I asked if I should put
the belt on, "No, if we need them, we'll put them on." I started to remember
what my father had said about flying. Sooner or later, all flyers will die. I said
I was cold; he said we'll get some heat when we get her up. I watched him
closely. He pushed the pedals and wobbled the stick. Leader did some other
things I couldn't comprehend. Prayerfully, he pressed a button that caused
the engine to struggle and shake the entire airplane, a slow semi-rotation of
the prop. I can remember that my Chevy had a similar ailment that could

be cured by connecting long cables to the battery and then connecting the other ends to another car. I couldn't imagine how you could connect two airplanes—I didn't have to. The oil delivery fellow backed an old truck out of the hangar, and you don't have to guess—it worked. The Chief started to clatter and sputter. Leader pushed a few more knobs and levers to smooth out the engine; my heart began to race faster than the engine.

Phil had been watching from the coffee room in the hangar. He waved at us while down the side road; we bumped around till we got to the end of the runway painted with the number 270. I wanted to ask what the number meant, but my speech was impaired by a lump in my throat. We went through a little drill, revved the engine, pushed the brakes in and out while waiting for the plane in front of us to take off. Leader hadn't said a thing, and as I sat there, with a burst of vocal agony, I asked, "What's this plane made of?" The answer was not supportive: "Canvas and paint," he said. Just then he turned the plane onto the runway and gunned the motor... the vibration was stirring. The motion was very slow at first, and finally, Leader pointed at the speed gauge and said,

"When it hits fifty, up we go"—and we did. I was
fixed on the fuel gauge, a
spindly wire bobbing up, down, and around
indicating about one-eighth full.
It has been said that just before death, your
entire life will flash before you. All
I could focus on was the day I ran out of gas, a
very rainy day. I had to walk
about two miles to get gas for the Chevy. The
airplane fuel gauge was close to
empty and I knew we couldn't walk now. The
shaking and shuttering seemed
to last for hours. As we went higher, I could see
some of the ground; the cars
looked like toys as I stared down. Leader said,
"Hold on." He turned the plane
sideways to turn left. I could see my knee
pressing on the canvas door. The
wind pushed us back as the plane twisted and
fought to keep flying. Over the
drone of the engine, I could hear my dad's words
ringing in my ears.

I could feel the engine heat now and I began to
smell something burning.
No sooner had the smell permeated the cabin
when smoke began pouring off
the engine. My mind was paralyzed; seconds
seemed like minutes—my entire
body was petrified; my mouth was too dry to
speak. An eerie sickness began
to twist my stomach as we oscillated from a left
turn into a steep climb.

Leader broke the silence and told me an airplane
that quits flying will go
into a stall.  I didn't question that—I just
accepted the notation and shook my
head.  My vocal cords were under seizure.
Leader said, "Put that seat belt on.
I want to show you a stall." I began fumbling, and
before I could finish, the
plane seemed to slow down with the nose high
and the wings wobbled… then
the end of the world. Leader pushed the stick
forward—the plane pointed
straight down like an arrow after a sparrow.
Nothing in my sixteen years of
life ever approached this—my father's words
rang and rang in my ears; then
as if grasped by God, the plane's nose began to
rise and we went back to a
steep climb. We continued to climb, then leveled
off—the smoke had stopped.
The fuel gauge still read one-eighth full and my
hands were dripping with
sweat. My mind erased the balance of the
lesson.

Experiences like this are never erased by time.
Speaking of time, about ten years later that old
urge began to push my sobering first flight
lesson into oblivion.  I couldn't resist the
conversations my friends were having about
their wonderful flying experiences.   "I'm going to
learn to fly". About 25 miles from my home was

an airport that advertised flying lessons. I had finished my sales call early one afternoon just as I passed the road to the airport. "Today's the day", I thought. I drove up to the reception area in front of the main hanger, took a deep breath, and walked right in. Between two partially repaired plane, a large man, chewing on a pipe, said, "What can I do for ya son"? My voice hadn't recovered from my last flying lesson ten years ago, but I managed - "Won't learn to fly". "You came to the right place". My vocal cords began to relax as we strolled around the hanger picking up old rags, tools and pans of oil - it reminded me of Mr. Painter's blacksmith barn without sparks. "Come over here - me learn a little more about ya son". I detected an English accent, "How's your health?
You look quite fit". "Here's the way we go about it"... he went into a show
and tell about the need to learn the flight rules, safety procedures and the absolute necessity of preflight procedures. "Let's go out here and go over this old Cub, show you what I mean". The Cub resembled the Chief right down to the canvas painted wings and oily old chunk of engine sticking out in front, and yes, that fuel gauge right up front. "Be careful yo don't trip over dat tie down rope". I already had while inspecting the wings for any sign of metallic support. Going back to the hanger I was watching a plane getting ready to land or crash. It hit the runway and then decided to take off again. Back in the rear of the hanger was a

coffee area with prominently posted licenses, official documents, and pictures of smiling pilots. "Here what it's going to cost and after you learn to fly you'll take a test and get your license. It all sounded reasonable.

I was just about to agree to the plan when he said, "I got to take care of this incoming plane. It's my wife, she's the instructor". Wife, instructor, all thoughts became tangled in a web of contemplation elevating my state of mental paralysis... a woman instructor... no way. Within 30 seconds I was in my car headed for home. No woman could possibly be safe to fly with. Look what happened to Amelia... A few miles down the road it suddenly struck me that another airport, where my friend kept his plane, was only a mile away. Half in shock, I drove up an old lane into large grassy area with five small planes perched along its edge. My friend, Art, was under his Skylane. A conversation ensued. He said, "When you gonna learn to fly?" I answered in haste asking him if anyone here taught flying. "You got to meet Vince. He got me flying. He just got a new Cherokee. He taught me to fly" Our conversation was interrupted by a little VW pulled in. "That's Vince. " "Hey Vince, here's a new student for you". Vince had arrived with another acquaintance of mine - there was an immediate social empowering group, clan, gathering, like a pride of lions...

I was in...

As things settled down I finished my log book beginners' entries and Vince said, "We're going to get you up right now. Here comes the Cherokee" The Cherokee pulled up right in front of the gas pump and as I looked over the new shinny plane, my confidence level soared like the stock market on steroids. I thought seeing a girl learning to fly minimized my lingering fear. A young girl, at that, looking about eighteen got out of the plane and came over to us. Vince said, "This is Cynthia, she's going to be your instructor today." I couldn't believe this was happening, thinking it a joke cooked up by my buddies... before I could react, Cynthia said, "Come over here, I'll show you how to gas her up". Yes, I did learn to fly with Cynthia and Vince's help.

My dad's basement was the focal point for budding radio and electronic geeks of the era. TV was not a household word or household item. Dad was a very serious, self-reliant person with a type A personality tinged with Irish independence. He had only attended school up to the eighth grade. He was put to work early to help the family. My grandfather was a literary type and well-known as a proofreader for publishing houses. It wasn't his purpose in life but that of circumstances. His father, my great-grandfather, was a country doctor, who treated my grandfather for a serious leg burn that never healed.

Grandpa was therefore relegated to a sitting position the balance of his life. I am not complaining or trying to explain my father's formal education. It was his determination that propelled him to self-educate. He took correspondence courses and drew upon books and personal experimentation for information.

He always said, and I still believe it to be true, "If you can read and use mathematics, you can perhaps understand or accomplish anything."

Dad's special insight and intuition became well-known, especially among the war veterans of the late forties. He began to experiment with microwave and frequency oscillation. Entrepreneurs and young veterans with forward-looking visions were regular visitors to my dad's workshop. Mother served them pie and coffee and I stood around and got in their way. I was also a magnet for followers in my own way. It was nearly a daily routine that friends met at my house to do high school homework—algebra, physics, and chemistry. I caught the entrepreneur spirit from the young veterans that congregated in our basement. Their focus on life was very special. These young men, most

only ten years my senior, influenced my course in life. Later, I recognized
that they were a source of great pleasure to my dad, who missed the war. It
was his contribution to the American effort and his contribution to a cause
he deeply believed in. During the war years, my life was adjusted to grief. I knew firsthand about the sorrow that wove through my neighborhood as the gold
stars were displayed.

Phil's dad and the older musicians in the area learned about my dance band
talent.   I started to play with some better-known orchestras and eventually
abandoned the Raindrops. That's the way it was—from sandlot free to starting
your own band then graduating to the majors.   I lost track of Phil for a while, later
learning that he never took his first flying lesson. Working with Phil's dad's orchestra, he told me his boy never did go flying. I suppose having seen me discharged from the little plane in a confused state of mind convinced Phil not to follow a flying future.
My mother's opinion of him was on the mark. I later saw him twitter
away his life. Up until this time, I always saw Phil with a grin on his face.
He could have been nicknamed Grin. He would never be without a portion

of the daily newspaper. I remember him reading for ten to fifteen seconds,
then raising his face with a big grin and giving a paraphrased account of the
subject. Phil liked to be known as an Irish leprechaun. His stature was small,
but his projection was ten feet tall. In truth he wasn't Irish. He believed his
adopted posture would elevate his chances of success, but it left him in the dust of progress.

My spirit was tainted by authentic Irish independence. I would question
Everything determined to understand the question and never expose
an answer to vague questions poised at the whim of educators. I demanded
a straight question. This attitude caused my academic evaluations to be
compromised. I suppose, in retaliation for my disruptive, challenging attitude,
instructors got the last laugh at grade time. I learned from this. It's taught in
law school—answer only the question in the shortest form possible and do
not volunteer any additional information. I also remember a Paul Newman
movie where he made an error in the cross-examination of a witness—"Never
ask a question that you do not already know the answer." Life is full of these
street-smart quips. I respect self-education. During high school, we are pushed

and prodded to enter college. We were spooked by teachers who only saw
the light in tunnels they had been lead into by books.  Over the years only a half dozen
teachers impressed me.  I was left with teachers with a shallow prospective of themselves unable to inspire their students.

God, grant us our leisure to appreciate the past.

After the end of World War II, things didn't return to be normal; they went
into an effervescing overdrive of expansion. No longer under the thumb of
the Great Depression, the business of the country was in the grip of great
expectation. We could never return to a normal or a simpler life.  I had been
the child of that Great Depression and now the prodigy of Great Expectation.
The country in 1933 was in a stable decline; the earth had left its orbit in the
late 1920s and roared into the wall of economic reality. It was at that moment
in time when the rebound, like a stretched tennis net, was strung between the
Axis and the Allies, waiting patiently for the game to begin.

I entered the Great Depression in 1936, when the country was just turning the corner in its struggle towards a stable economy.  It was at that moment

in time when the greed and vanity of nations
captured the better judgment
of humanity.  I would like to have been older
than three in 1938, perhaps
fourteen, to have caught the reality of life during
the worst of times; but with
that wish, I would have faced the risk of being
killed in World War II.  Those
gold stars were indeed reality.  The USS
Sullivan, a US Naval cruiser, was
commissioned near the end of the war to honor
the five Sullivan brothers
who were killed in the South Pacific.  I can't
imagine the stinging reality of
placing five gold stars in the window of my
home.  I was at war when I was just starting first
grade.   I was in a war of sorts, the fear of
authority and the intimidation hurled at me by a
ruthless old maid.  I was suffering childhood post
traumatic stress syndrome shot by a bottom
order pecker first grade teacher.

I can remember the first day of school...

The sun was just peeking through our back
porch.  Standing in front of a mirror on the back
porch, on a cooler than normal September
morning, my mother was adjusting my brown suit
and beanie cap.  The beanie cap had a leather
snout with a button on the top which mother was
sewing tightly that morning.  I watched my
mother nervously thread a needle.  It seemed
she made a thousand attempts to get the needle

threaded. I watched her hands. They had an unusual tremor as she wove the needle through the loop in the button, like a little girl just beginning to sew. She groped for the loop and the button, missing the hole repeatedly. It seemed her apprehension of me going to school completely blocked her skills as a seamstress. I had watched her many times as she sewed with great agility and skill, but the sun through the window seemed to blind her ability. I remember staring at the segmented seams that radiated from the button of the top of the cap into what looked like freshly cut cinnamon-covered pumpkin pie with a snout. My mother repeatedly took it on and off, straightening my hair, but I really didn't care. I felt cold that morning, and I really didn't want to go to the first day of school. In September, the sun's angle at 7:00 AM is quite low. It was a clear day, and the sun came through the curtain on the back porch window and reflected off the fluted edges of the mirror. It broke the sun's rays into a rainbow at each little flute. I seemed to be mesmerized by the rainbow effect, which appears as vividly today as it did over seventy years ago. My tears began as my mother made her exit from the room. I have always been trying to forget that first day of school. I am reminded by present circumstances that freedom is a mythical compartment of your mind. There is no such reality. You always find yourself locked into a semi-solitary cell of confinement. That's the way humanity treats itself.

As my grade school confinement advanced - the war overseas ended. Music opened my cell door.  This was an enlightening distraction from the wars... music opened me to self expression. Up until piano lesson time, I had been able to handle most crises with an acceptable standard of conduct. Mrs. Glover, my piano teacher lived in a small house in my neighborhood.  It had an unusual odor. Could it have been that my lesson was always on a Thursday and that she prepared the same lunch every Thursday? I could have been blindfolded with two steps inside the door and I would have known precisely where I was and what day it was. I could walk to her home,  but I usually rode my mother's bicycle, which I had fitted with a small chain wrapped around the back wheel for extra traction in the winter.  It was a good idea but basically impractical. A bicycle has a mind of its own, like man, with snow on the ground.
Mrs. Glover was a plump old lady. She looked old then but would have been
younger than me now.  Just like the smell of her house, she wore the same dress
every Thursday or perhaps every day, as far as I know.  It was a faded grayish
white dress, almost matching her hair with a pattern of sprinkled blue pansies.
She seemed to have a student every half hour because someone was always leaving when I was arriving, and someone was always arriving when I was leaving.  I never knew these people

intimately. In fact, some never even spoke because I never met their age standard or some other standard for that matter. Just like passing ships in the night, we never amassed ourselves until that one day out of the year for the annual right of passage - recital.

It was 7 PM on a late June evening and Mrs. Glover was conducting the agonies of the annual right of passage. I had been taking lessons for three years, and each year required a recital to entertain the parents. This ordeal brought my mind and spirit to a state of compressed apprehension. Well, tonight's the night... when 14 students attempted to justify the cost reward ratio for the lessons and the intimidation of peer review pecking order. We were seated in isolation from the audience when the girl next to me asked, "What note does your song start on?" The knot in my stomach tightened. The juices in my throat nearly choked me. I couldn't think. My mind ran helplessly in a thousand directions. It was hot, and I was sweating. I can't even remember her name. She was a pain-in-the-ass (Pain) brat. I saw her once a year. She seemed to have a tongue that was mechanically attached to a gramophone. She talked continuously. I was the next to deliver my recital when the "Pain" asked me for a second time, what note my piece began with. I went numb, even my nose. I couldn't smell a thing. In fact, I wasn't sure I was in Mrs. Glover's house. I was mortified like a petrified log with two petrified limbs. I moved through the curtain out to the piano. I sat in front of middle C and my mind was a total blank. I couldn't see, smell, hear, or think. I knew my ears were on fire. I was afraid to touch them for fear they would burst into flames. My heart pounded like old Mr. Painter's sledgehammer on hot steel. I can still remember old Mr. Painter, the blacksmith, pounding and heating pieces of metal. The sparks were flying with every blow of the hammer. I couldn't swallow. It seemed like an eternity of seconds until Mrs. Glover half-crawled from behind the audience, and I heard her whisper, "What's the matter?" Miraculously my vocal cords relaxed enough to say, "I can't remember how it starts." She said, "Where is your music?" I said, "I left it at home because I know it." She said, "Then play it". I continued to stare at middle C, and I began to smell that Thursday smell again emanating from Mrs. Glover's nostrils. She was somewhat snorting like an old cow or bull that was ready to charge. I was distracted by the droplets of water in her breath, polka-dotting my glasses. I suppose the pressure of that moment has affected my life in many ways. Perhaps it has helped me cope with my not-so-successful charge into the sunset on my old Hummer motorcycle (to

be covered later), or was it life's annual dose of adrenaline to test our genes
and DNA, or could it be that my gorilla experience (to be covered later) kept
me from a total meltdown in front of middle C. I believe this was my first
religious experience as God rescued me. My thumbs were directed to middle
C and then spread by divine intervention to a G chord, and I was suddenly
released from my agony. Piano lessons were suspended after the recital giving
our malleable little minds time to heal during the summer. Your torture would
subside over the coming months in preparation for the next right of passage.

My place in the universe forever…

Before the beginning of the Second World War, my father purchased a 1939
Hudson.  He was a visionary and figured we would be in a war soon.  He was right about getting a new car to replace the Model A Ford. The Great Depression had nearly ended as world turmoil indicated that we might be into a war lasting for years. Dad's instincts proved correct and he traded the model A on a new 1939 Hudson.   I remember riding home in the new Hudson and looking down at the scab on my leg still healing from trying to break a wheel nut loose on the model A.  I disliked the model A. It was crude, noisy, slow and culturally deficient.

Fortunately, the Hudson didn't have a foot-operated wheel wrench. I loved the Hudson. The Hudson's charisma wore thin over the war years, as did the paint. I didn't realize until I started to associate with the other side of the tracks that very few households were self-sufficient. Dad took it upon himself to correct any malfunction at home himself. We took responsibility for wiring the house, repairing the plumbing, painting the house, repairing furniture, etc. It was next to sacrilege to hire anyone to do things you could do yourself, even if you didn't know how. I can frankly say that my dad didn't find fun in his life as defined by society. The world tries to define us and I have always believed that my father was trying to break out of that definition. Putting a demand on his potential fueled his life. Dad firmly believed that he could do anything and after a little practice, he did with fair amount of skill I might add. If the hot water tank broke, he fixed it. If a fuse blew, he rewired it. Now, many of these jobs required special tools. Our basement and garage were literally crammed with specialized tools ranging from an air compressor to electronic test equipment. My dad was no amateur. As I look about my community and see many successful inventors and engineers who, when they were in their early twenties, sought my dad out, picking his brain, so to speak for information. I can speak for these budding inventors. It was the simple pleasure of looking over my dad's shoulders that captivated their imagination; he made it a game to experiment with electrical phenomena. I always considered him somewhat of a low-level Einstein.

I can remember one of my father's "middle C meltdowns". The war years of wear and tear on the Hudson pointed to the hasty blending of paint the factory used in 1939. By 1946, the paint was peeling and the cosmetics appeal of the Hudson couldn't be tolerated by my father. You guessed it. We painted the Hudson at home. Now, painting the Hudson is like painting any other car, I suppose. But when my father decided to do something, the plan would be completely outlined and copies distributed among the participants so that the project would go without a hitch. Note, I was the only participant and it was my job to sand off the old paint. This required using files, wire brushes, sand paper, steel wool, and elbow grease. My dad must have thought I had more elbow grease than I had since the project was lingering on. The pace of preparing the car for painting was interrupted on a daily basis by my father's work schedule. That meant everyone in town knew that the Hudson was under restoration. A fender at a time with a little primer here and there gave the Hudson a military look. The pace of this procedure began to defeat itself. By the time we got from one side of the car to the other, new rust was beginning to form and in a desperate attempt to finish the job, my father hired two of my young friends to help me finish. By Saturday afternoon all was going well. We were cutting pieces of newspaper and taping them onto the windows and masking the little chrome letters that spelled "Hudson". We had to spray the entire garage with water so that there wouldn't be any dust in the air. My father planned to attack the Hudson with paint at precisely 7:00 PM. He had strung extra lighting throughout the garage, had loaded his new Devilbiss spray gun, which he had caressed for several days getting the feel of its trigger, adjusting the spray nozzle and reading excessively about the art of painting. A little after seven, the Hudson was backed into the garage. Its tires and wheels were covered with blankets and a final piece of tape wrapped around the door handle. Like a man from outer space, my father had his respirator on to keep from breathing the paint fumes, and then he said, "Everybody out.". The painting had begun. We tried to look through the garage windows, but within seconds, our vision was fogged with an enormous cloud of paint swirling about the Hudson. The only way we could tell my father was still in action in the war with the paint was an occasional shadowing of a bright light as his arms swung wildly like the Michelangelo of auto painting. After about thirty minutes, my mother came out of the house, looked through the garage window, and screamed that my dad must have collapsed having lost the war with the paint. Just as she was about to open the door,

my father looked out of the window.   He looked
like a gun metal gray Martian peering out of his
spaceship.  His glasses were smeared and he
was covered with paint. After about an hour
when the smoke had cleared, I opened the door
to retrieve the paint gun so that we could clean it
up and get it ready for the next paint job.  My
dad had taken a bath in paint solvent by this time
and he looked pretty good.  My short glimpses of
the Hudson led me to believe that this was
another family success story.


I have often been bothered by my awareness of
anxieties like picking the petals from a daisy—
she loves me, she loves me not—or some other
mystical precursor of the destiny we humans
strive to foresee.  I suppose the words echo in
my ear today, "Don't go into the garage until
tomorrow morning. You don't want to stir up the
dust and speckle the car."  The tension created
by the anxiety to gloat over the successful
restoration of the Hudson was almost more than
I could bear. I finally fell asleep about 11:00 PM,
Saturday night with visions of a gleaming gun
metal gray Hudson (3737 the Hudson's nick
name, after the last four digits of its serial
number) rolling down the highway—faster than a
speeding bullet, more powerful than a
locomotive and able to leap small mountains in a
single bound.  Those were the days when kids
like me were impressed by radio programs
featuring Captain Midnight, the Lone Ranger and

Superman. The apprehension of waiting for our cornflake box top's secret decoding device to come in the mailbox was like telling yourself that you were not going to throw up in reverse at every disappointing visit to the mailbox. Each repeated trip to the mailbox was another petal from the daisy. This is part of our training as children, for life is filled with petal picking. Somewhere in my college training, I read the life of Albert Einstein. I know how he must have felt presenting E=mc2 to his peers. It was probably a cross between a "middle C meltdown" and a fumble on a ride into the sunset—like your foot slipping off a model A wheel wrench at the speed of a bullet gliding along the shaft of the wrench. I remember
how that felt. Even though the velocity of your limb seems instantaneous, the pain lingers for hours and depending upon the pressure of the exercise, the scab may not disappear for months. Perhaps it is the true scientific method by which all standards are derived. I can just visualize Albert writing x=A3, y=B3, z=C3 . . . and out of some miraculous intuitive energy, suddenly E=mc2. It could have been a leap from faith to reality, or was it an implantation from a higher power? Many like to believe that we mortals have all had a parallel universal preexistence and now we float from planet to planet in our spiritual beings and swoop down in the moment of conception taking command of some little body, only to be spit out into the world as an Einstein or Carpenter.

Remember, Robert Burns said, "The best laid plans of mice and
men are subject to adjustment". Well, I think that's the best way to finish the
Hudson story. For some reason, I had slept longer than usual and when
I awoke, my unconsciousness had been preoccupied with something
other than the Hudson overnight. It was late summer and the tomatoes
were just beginning to ripen. I loved tomatoes and still do. I used to
help my grandmother plant them. Planting tomatoes was another major
family project, and I had a habit of picking petals from life's daisy
drawer, counting the days, and watching the tomatoes grow so I could
bite into those luscious orange-striped green fruits of my labor. I got
dressed and took the dog with me. We went immediately next door to
my grandmother's house looking for tomatoes. My grandmother told
me never to eat a tomato unless it had at least a few orange stripes on
it. I had been watching one in particular and with all of the activity
the day before, prepping the Hudson for paint, I had forgotten to check
the tomato. I went immediately into the garden and sure enough, the

tomato was ready.  As I grabbed it, it occurred to me that I hadn't checked

out the Hudson yet.  What a fantastic day, I thought.   My first tomato of

the season, and we can untape the Hudson today and take a ride up the

mountain.  I was so excited I couldn't stand it.  I wanted to pull all of the

petals from the daisy right then and there.  How good would it look?  I

ran in the house, through the kitchen, rinsed my tomato, and salted it

well, ran down through the cellar and took a bite out of my tomato;

and just as the juices of the tomato entered my mouth and swirled over

my tongue and taste buds, I swung open the cellar garage door.  I can't

remember that I ever swallowed.  I couldn't believe it.  My mouth was

beginning to fill with juices, a precursor to regurgitation.  I took several

steps closer to the Hudson.  It looked like a giant alligator.  Its skin had

crinkled and cracked and creviced.  I left the garage and went into the

cellar blinking. I couldn't believe it.  I took another look.  It wasn't an

alligator; it was the Hudson.  My father was asleep.  How should I tell him

about the transformation of the Hudson into an alligator?  A few minutes

went by and I began to wonder what standard
had I abused. Did I open
the door too soon? Did the vapors from the
tomato suddenly penetrate
the paint and cause it to react in a violent and
transforming manner? I
don't know what happened to the tomato. I don't
remember eating it or
throwing it away. Perhaps the first bite
disintegrated in my mouth from
the toxic juices generated by my physic vision at
the transformed Hudson.
I have a lapse of memory as to what happened
just after my father woke
up and inspected the Hudson. I later found out
that mixing lacquer
thinner and enamel paint was the problem. I
suppose my father's "middle
C meltdown" was so violent, next to a nuclear
collapse, that the radiating
energy had numbed the memories of everyone
within several blocks of
our house.

Then winter set in…

I decided to ask dad about airplanes a few
weeks after my flying sweat in. I
said, "Hey, Dad, did you ever go flying?" Dad
never liked to answer without
considering all the ramifications of his answer.
He said, "What brings up this

subject?" He didn't wait for an answer, then said, "I told you it is not safe."
"Well, how do you know if you haven't done it?"
Now the admission: he said,
"I took a ride in a kite." I said, "What kind of kite?" "It was a Ford trimotor . . .
never again. What a cheap heap of junk. I was sort of trapped into the ride. "
"When I was working as a scab (worker who won't unionize) in Allentown,
Pennsylvania, some of the other scabs got together and hired a ride. That's
what I mean about mixing with the wrong people. You get sucked into doing
things you wouldn't do on your own." I suppose, now that I reflect on my
relationships, my dad was spot-on when he said, "Be careful who you associate
with." In Greek history the Trojan horse story is a good example. You should
consider unwelcomed generosity as an obligation to be collected in the future.

I was itching for more spending money, a faster car, and a notch up on my
peers. I was lucky when I got acquainted with Wally—that was her name. She
lived on the same street as the high school and would put two old chairs out on
the street to save me a high-valued parking place. This arrangement, although
twisted by circumstances, led to my after school job at Ken Howard's garage.

I think the details here are irrelevant; the bottom
line was my experiences
with the English immigrant, Ken Howard. He was
a mechanic extraordinaire,
bringing secrets from across the ocean that
transformed common Fords into
speed demons.


The three Bs were Ken's principal customers—
notice I did not use the spelling
of the word principal as principle, they were used
car dealers—not to be
construed as principled men. Two things
motivated Ken—making money
and winning stock car races. Perhaps I
overvalued the making of money—it
was more about winning races. Ken introduced
me to tricks and shortcuts in
auto service, resulting in making faster money to
support the racing. Yes, it
is true, you can mix sawdust with gear oil and
stop the whining of a worn axel or
transmission. That was my specialty; I could
slither under the cars without
jacking them up and do the oil treatment. This
tricky procedure took place
in the Tenth Street alley. The alley had a
concave shape and when the old
Buicks were straddling the ditch, I could easily
do the oil treatment. I never
had the opportunity at this early stage in my life
to even say hello to Mr. Big

"B," the one with the long camel hair coat and a perfumed aftershave lotion
that infected every car he ever drove.  Mr. "B" and his two accomplices, both
with the last name beginning with a capital B, they drove Packard's, big ones
'48 Super Clippers. You would think they would all have been black—they
were all light green, kind of foamy surf green with big white tires.

Mr. Big "B" must have recognized me at one of the clubs I played with Jack
Baker's Band.  The following Monday, he told Ken to send me over.  He wanted
to talk to me. "You're a pretty classy kid," he said. "Do you have a car?" "Yea,
a '33 Chevy." "That's it over there?" "OK, here's my card. Go down to Charlie's
tire shop, and he will put four new white tires on it.  I love that song, St. Louie
Blues, play it for me and my buddies when your see us come into the club."  I didn't answer,
stunned by the generosity. He turned and drove off in his Packard. A few days later, my dad
asked about the tires. I told him the story and that was like striking a match in the gas tank.
Dad blew his top. Bang! "What did you have to do to get the money for them?" I said, "Play St
Louie Blues every time he came into the club." This ignited a further explosive blow off from
Dad.  "I

don't like you playing in those joints—all a bunch
of no-good boozers. If I ever
catch you taking even a taste, that's it, that's it,
we're finished." I was about to
turn seventeen now and my parents' focus was
on my going to college. They
wanted me to be their doctor in their old age or
be the doctor that my great
grandfather could have been if not for the
alcohol.

This was a hard formula to adapt while working
at Ken's from three till seven after school and
playing in the band from ten till one. It would
seem that my parents would have not permitted
this—but oh, to the contraire, my dad worked for
enjoyment. He didn't have any other interests
outside of work—it defined him. He always
seemed to be pushing for the next job or
challenge, small challenges that he valued in
conquering, to define himself, to set himself
apart from those who were limited in scope. I
look back now and understand his self-revealing
pursuits; however, there were those moments so
well framed by Robert Burns.

It was not certain to me or anyone in the
neighborhood what would happen
if America lost the war, and in fact, my
impression was that America would
probably lose. It wasn't difficult even to a second
grader to interpret the

conversations. It was a weekly occurrence for
the gold star to appear in some
new house in the town. Two gold stars were
uncommon, but two sons lost
to the war were terrifying. There is a circle of
dogwood trees in the front lot
of my old elementary school. After the end of the
war, a tribute was made
for the young men who attended the school who
never came back, killed
in the line of duty. To this day, I ponder the big
one, that's what they called
it, the big one and all the little and not-so-little
wars since—why greed and
vanity hold man hostage to the logistics of
economics. Memories are short,
and the gold stars and dogwood trees are but a
shadow now; the logistics of
life persist.

Life is full of logistics. Most people fail to use
them. I never had enough money
to use them. Take heed, everything is economic
and logistics are your tickets
to economic independence.  It was in the early
1940s when this fact made its
first impression on me. The Second World War
was raging and those too
young to go to war, this included me, or those
too old were stranded in time
waiting for it to be all over.

There was an old blacksmith shop just out of
walking distance from me, closer
to town where my dad took me to have parts
repaired and pieces made. Old
Mr. Painter was forging metal and beating red
sparks for at least fifty years
before I met him. I didn't matter to him, but he
mattered to me enough for
the both of us. I was fascinated with what he
could do and impressed that my
dad handed him money. Everyone was giving
him money for beating red hot
sparks and spitting black juice on the floor.
Maybe that's why he was called a
blacksmith, I thought.  Halfway between
Painter's and my house was Horner's
Chicken Farm.  On occasion, I would ride along
with my friend, whose father
was the chicken farmer. A trip to the city
delivering chickens was something
like the blacksmith business—you hammer out
the iron pieces and you cut
off the chickens' heads and you get money for
this.

While the war was still going on, there was
another kind of black business.
It was called the black market. Not because
everyone was spitting black juice
on the floor like Mr. Painter, but because it had a
lot to do with tires and
those tires were always black. I later found out
that this black business was

as logical as life—you give them money and they give you black tires. There
was rationing during the war. Those who stayed at home were not allowed
to have things even if they had money. There was the effort to win the big
one and it took everyone's commitment to that end and many took it a few
steps farther by helping out with the black market so that the home folks
could have what they didn't need. Logistics, hey! This idea of getting people to
give you money began to make sense to me by the time I went to high school.
It was preordained that I should be a physician. It was apparent to my parents
that the physicians were getting more than their share, judging by the cars they drove. I was beginning to see their point. Cars always had a special place in my life. They had human features and smiles or frowns. Some looked fast, some sounded fast, and the new ones smelled better than any of my mother's perfume. I became an expert at identifying them by their sound. The Buicks had a squealing first gear that gave them away, and the starters on Fords were easy pickings. John Morton had a 1939 Chrysler, a neat country club green. I would time his movements just to get a look at it. John was a carpenter who did a few
small jobs helping my dad finish our house and any time John was helping,

I was inspecting every feature of that Chrysler. I would slide in behind
the steering wheel and drive off in my mind's eye to far corners. Once, in
an altered state of mind, I touched the starter, and the Chrysler jumped
forward in a lurch, smacking me back to reality. I was breathless for a few
seconds. I never touched the Chrysler again. I didn't trust myself.  Pretend
driving is a wonderful way to lull you to sleep. I would just lie back and
put it in gear and sail away.

Back at Ken Howard's garage, stock car racing began to consume most of our
time. Taking care of the three Bs' used cars was crowding the racing effort.
After about three months on the job at Ken's, I would be a regular part of
the pit crew—it was me and Ray, another local hot-rodder. I was itching to
get a chance to drive that car around the track. I kept asking Ken to let me
warm it up. Week after week I kept pushing the issue. "OK, Davy, give her
a lap." My chance came during an afternoon event early in May 1953. I was
stunned at first. I began to seize up just like my first flying lesson. Ken told
me to stay inside the half-mile oval and not to get mixed up with the hotshots

who were practicing. The pit was inside the oval track area, so entering the

raceway would be the slowest and safest place to get up to speed. "Now, just

do a lap and come back in, got it? Stay on the inside. Don't give anyone

enough room to get inside your line, got it? Watch that bump at the entrance

to the pit road. Got it?" I was sitting in front of two other cars waiting to

practice. Ken's Ford was a 1937 coupe with a late model flat head Mercury

ABA. They were revving their engines and bumping me up to get out on

the track. I didn't plan anything at this point. Before I knew, I was going for

second gear and being passed and bumped all over the track. The Ford went

into a side-skidding maneuver that propelled me up to the outside groove

in with the fast cars. I hit the gas pedal to keep from getting run over. I was

moving blindly as the dirt and wads of mud pelted my face through the open

windshield—only a wire mesh screen kept the big stuff from killing me. I was

being battered around by the other cars. The roar of their open exhaust, the

smoke, the dust, and the bashing I was taking went on for about three laps.

I was looking for the inside lane and pit entrance. I had to get off the track.

I spotted the pit lane and dove down towards it
only to be broadsided by a
bigger car. I straightened the car out on the next
lap and finally got back to
our space. Ken said, "I told you one lap." I knew
the way he said it I could never go back to Ken's
garage. The experience is still sketchy; it truly
scared me. I can only remember the stark terror.
I felt like a Christian who was thrown to the lions
and lived to tell about it. I have since theorized
that this experience, like going over Niagara
Falls in a barrel, has contributed to my fear of
enclosed, tight places. I do not, to this day, enjoy
elevators, or closed places.


"Stop . . . stop it, for Christ's sake, where's your
brain, boy?"  "This is just about
the end of your driving.  Can't you see what
could happen if you injured someone exiting a
bus or street car when it's stopped.  What if
someone had stepped out in front of you—bam!
you'd have flattened him.  It's hard enough
making a living without going out and acting
stupid." Dad went on and on saying that
If you'd hit someone like that, your mother and
I'd be sued, probably lose the house. The
lawyers would eat us up. The streetcars ran on
rails up the middle of the street with enough
room to have regular and opposing traffic go on
either side of the streetcar. Sometimes the
streetcar would make a close turn and the laws
of geometry would be enforced whether or not

your car was in the way. Crunch! The arc made by the streetcar would squeeze a traffic jammed car and usually press some nasty dents and creases into the car's fenders and doors. "Now, don't stop here.  Move up next to that Ford. Go on, get a little closer. If that streetcar comes around, you don't want to be clipped by its ass end."

I wasn't allowed to drive for a month - till my dad got over my stupid
spell.  The message from Dad lingers in my mind now over fifty years later.
I had visions of throwing a pedestrian over into the next county as he stepped
from a streetcar. "Just try to get any money out of the city. They'll fiddle you
around for years. Then their smart lawyers will blame it on you. For Christ's
sake, don't give 'em an inch, or they'll take a mile. You're never going to beat
city hall. The governments got you licked before you start. That's their job."
"The Japanese, the treacherous bastards, walked into the White House and
schmoosed Roosevelt and that dummy let them bomb Pearl Harbor the very
next day. When is America going to wake up and take the first shot?"  "No,
the government has their way, but if you bump into one of their streetcars,
you'll pay."  Dad had a way of expressing his innermost thoughts sometimes

without considering the consequences or the opinion generated by his Irish
aggressive independence, but that was Dad. What is it, they say? "The apple doesn't fall far from the tree".

I was dad's official gofer and light holder.  I suppose my concept of
standards began here.  "Pay attention," my dad snapped. "Point the light right
here where I am working. Keep your mind on what I am doing.  Pay attention
and don't be gazing all over the theater or we will be here all night."  At that
instant, I realized that the rest of my life would somehow be imposed upon
by a standard for something or other.  Standards had been corrupted during
the Second World War. Winning the war was the standard for America. Any
standard that got in the way would be trampled, bent, or crushed without
recourse since the end justified the means. Dad said, "Get the big box." My
pulse immediately shifted to second gear as I took the flashlight and walked
through the old Penn Theater, out the back door, into the alley where the
old Hudson was parked full of electricians' tools and supplies. That
Hudson felt secure like a tank; a refuge to me because it resembled

one of the military staff cars I would see in the wartime movie newsreels.  It
was the halfway point where I could collect my composure and take a deep
breath before going back through the scary old theater. The old Penn Theater
had been used for stage performances and was closed during the war. The
emergency light system had to be maintained monthly along with a dozen
other theaters in my hometown that Dad had contracted to service.
The big box carried BX cable, fiber bushings, alcohol for the soldering torches,
friction tape and electrical box binders. The carrying cable would stretch with
each step I took under the weight. It was a heavy load that I barely managed
since I had to walk between the prop section and the stage to the stairs into
the basement.  I still can't get over the stuffed gorilla on wheels. I knew it
was there, along with the other stuffed animals. I was petrified. Today I can feel the knot in my stomach as I think about it.  I suppose that my little trip to get the big box was another standard of sorts that I must conform to.  There were times I wished I could have stayed inside the security of the old Hudson.

Years later I needed another car...

You could tell by the table that either a late
breakfast or an early lunch was
in the process at the Burd family. I was
immediately preoccupied by Jimmy's
distorted left eye. You know, it was the kind of
thing that you didn't ask about,
but every second of my visit, like a magnetic
force I stared at Jim's eye. There
were coffee cups half-filled or partially consumed
strewn about the kitchen
and I knew they were going to ask me if I wanted
a cup of coffee.  I presumed
they had used every coffee cup that they owned.
One of the half-filled cups
was taken from the countertop, dumped in the
sink and quickly rinsed out
for my portion of the blackest, thickest Maxwell
House coffee ever
created. I turned my cup around, to the cleanest
side, pretending to be left-
handed, avoiding the dirty side of the cup.  I
realized that I was again staring
into Jimmy's damaged and distorted eye.  His
mother realized my attraction
and sought to ease my staring. She related the
story of Jimmy's second day
on the job at the railroad shops when a drill bit
shattered, piercing his safety
glasses and blinding his left eye for life. Years
later, just as I was being seated,
I looked across the restaurant; there it was
again. Only one eye in this world

could look like that. It hadn't changed, but the body that was carrying it around
had gained about a hundred pounds and lost a few thousand hairs. Unmistakably, it was Jimmy. I couldn't think of his last name, but the circumstances were under perfect recall in my memory. It has been more than forty years since I paid my visit to the Burd family that Saturday morning. My purpose had to do with buying a dilapidated old Nash Ambassador from his mother. This old blue bathtub had a smashed front fender with the headlight dangling precariously to the bumper. I can remember Jimmy taking me to the backyard with a battery and an assortment of petroleum distillates that were intended to charm the beast into life. Then I realized that Jimmy was staring at me from across the restaurant and I could detect that he knew me yet didn't know why. I went over and said to him, "Jimmy, do you remember the old Nash?" He burst into a roaring laughter that turned every head in the restaurant. He said, "Do you remember when the carburetor caught on fire?" I said, "Well, I remember scooping up handfuls of wet snow trying to put it out." I sat with Jimmy for a time, and we reminisced about that December morning—the same kind of morning,
just like today.

I remember some fellows at school doing their double takes when I first

parked the old Nash behind the dorm. I had
taped the headlight back in place.
Looking like a wounded veteran that it was, the
old Nash drew many curious
snickers and comments; but for $175, this Nash
would mean freedom to me.
During the next few weeks, I corrected most of
its problems by getting used
parts from a local salvage lot. In those days,
when you needed used auto parts,
you had to do the job twice. You were instructed
by the junk yard's owner to
take your own tools out into the muddy, snowy
yard and remove the parts you
needed from the derelicts; then take them home
with you and put them on.
The home garage to me was the back parking lot
of the dorm. In spite of the
fact that the temperature had dropped to ten
degrees with a stiff wind, within
what seemed like weeks, I brought the old Nash
to an acceptable mechanical
standard, and that standard was difficult to meet
since I had been raised to
respect standards for the last twenty years at
home.

I drove back to my office after Jimmy and I had
swapped stories about cars
and motorcycles, and with a fresh cup of coffee,
I found myself recalling how
scared I was carrying the big box through the
desolate old Penn Theater. The

big box was always called for when the job was about half-finished. I can still
see the box. It had a thick, rubber-encased no. 10 extension wire line knotted
on both ends to secure it to what was once a pop bottle carton. I took a sip from my coffee and found it was cold. It startled me. How long had I been daydreaming? It was cold outside.  I'm accustomed to cold, but
never grew fond of it.  Pennsylvania has its share of both hot and cold,
but Pennsylvania is mostly a cold state.  I suppose the Scots, Irish, Poles, and
Germans settled in Pennsylvania because it mirrored the climate and terrain
of their homeland.  It seems inconceivable that my relatives would have engaged war in such deadly and treacherous temperatures.  Is this some standard
to which humans conform?  I threw my cold coffee away and went home.

Cushman ( middle "C" meltdown)

About 250 years ago Great Britain began to cast off its unsophisticated residents from Ireland and Scotland… they migrated to America settling in the small towns and forests of Appalachia. Communities, named after their abandoned homes like Tyrone, Donegal, Birmingham, Bedford and Surry, popped up in little river bottoms, obscured forests and quiet valleys. The instinct of these people had been carried across the Atlantic and their heritage could be seen in the construction of their homes and workplaces. There is a small nearby town that resembles Northern England as does the climate and the single fascination for motorized bicycles. These people working hard had a curious hoarding, type-wad mentality akin to the thrift of the Scots and the foolishness of the Irish. It was here I found a remarkable descendent, Delmar, a craftsman, part artist and engineer who spent most of his time caring for a brood of Cushman motor scooters.

I first met Delmar a few days after Christmas. Delmar had a straight forward style. I found his garage in a muddy alley behind several old vehicles in some state of repair or disrepair. I opened the garage door and was immediately taken by the ongoing projects Delmar was working on. I could see that his artistic talent and crafty engineering defined this fellow. He immediately led me into a staggering room full of finished Cushman motor scooters, shelves of old parts each with an identity tag of great detail. He said, "Here's my Cushman Silver Eagle. I set it up for the national drags last year." Delmar pointed out that he remodeled the engine and transmission in great detail. The time with Delmar passed quickly and he invited me to his house for coffee and more exciting Cushman scooters.

He began by giving the Cushman history in the USA. From 1936-1966 the Cushman Motor Works of Lincoln, NE built motor scooters. Their original intention was not to build motor scooters but to increase sales of their engines. The Cushman Co. was an engine manufacturer that catered to the agricultural and material handling industry. Their reputation for building good reliable engines gave them a head start in marketing their scooters. They were, in fact, the biggest scooter manufacturer in the USA. At the beginning, the USA was in the midst of the Great Depression when the first scooters were built. The appeal of cheap transportation was tempered only by the lack of money to buy them. Sales were never brisk until after WWII. Sales shot up the economic bell curve peaking in 1954 and ending in 1966. Most of Delmar's scooters are from the peak years but his restored military version is a sight to see. This military scooter built in Nebraska was transported across the USA, shipped thru the U-boat infested north Atlantic to England, loaded into a C47, and then parachuted to the coast of France on D-Day. It was apparently ridden for 18 months under siege of war, then smuggled back to the USA when it was all over. Delmar makes the difference when you are in the midst of history as he puts his collection in a virtual reality smack in your face. He can weave you thru New York traffic on his 1946 Cushman with the perspective skill of Shakespeare. After listening to Delmar's account of his scooter rides, you can experience

his cold, numb hands as he winds his way
through a freezing rain storm, feel the back
snapping pain of piloting his Silver Eagles over
cobblestone streets. But the real magic comes
later on as you imagine an America with $5 a
gallon gas and a populous forced to ride more
scooters.

You begin to see yourself working your way
through traffic on your trusty Cushman making
fools of four wheelers at every stop light as
Delmar finishes his tale about riding the annual
Cushman Jamboree. I found myself lusting to
go back across the Atlantic to my ancestral
origins scooter-touring the ancient turf (on the
wrong side of the road) imagining zooming up to
Stone Henge peering through the huge stones
for my past. It must be great to take the mid
summer ride along the coast to Blackpoll then
run up thru Ireland (kiss the Blarney Stone) then
on across Scotland for a bit of haggis. Sorry, but
I would rather settle for a Big Mac. Recovering
from Delmar's Cushman spell, it was easy to
understand his devotion to these clever two
wheelers.

The Cushman Scooter was the liberator of
youth...a magic carpet to the future. Their
advertising justified the scooter as a workhorse
that loved to frolic with its owner while delivering
newspapers or running to the grocery store for
mom's order. You could lie in bed, read the ads
and then ride off into your mind's eye as you fall

asleep with sweet dreams of your next Cushman adventure. Youth is complicated in America. There is peer pressure, cheap gasoline and overproduction of motor cars all subsidized by the government's cheap credit folly. By the 1950's, a fast used Ford could be bought for $300 and a new Cushman cost $400. The Ford would carry six and gave you plenty of room for romance. The end had come for Cushman's middle C meltdown in 1966.

My First Harley…

"What is that thing out there?" "What thing?" "That thing you rode up on?". I told him it was a Harley Hummer. Everybody roared when Bill said, "Where's the rest
of it?" Well, I didn't stay more than five seconds after that remark. I simply
slithered across the shop and tried to bring my piece of dirt motorcycle to
life with one kick and ride smartly off into the sunset, but it took a series of
kicks, curse words, and fumbling with the carburetor to bring it to life; and
instead of riding off into the sunset, it simply died a few yards away from
his front door. In my haste to leave, I forgot to turn the fuel tap on. The
laughter still echoes in my mind as I obviously didn't meet some standard I
was not aware of yet. This little old three-car garage had been the motorcycle

Mecca for twenty years with Nortons, BSAs,
BMWs, Ariels, and an occasional
off-brand like a Harley became temporarily
respectable because it shared
garage space with the "in crowd" of
motorcycling.

Bill was a master mechanic and between the
Pabst Blue Ribbon and his worst enemy,
himself, he threw in the towel selling me his
business twenty five years later and retired to
Phoenix. The first time I met Bill, I was riding a
little Harley Hummer, and he and his cronies just
laughed me off as it was not in the thoroughbred
arena of his clientele. But I was young,
seventeen, and lucky to have any wheels, let
alone two wheels. But as time went on, Bill and I
became friends, even though I was his
competitor for a number of years. Bill only stayed
in Phoenix a year—long enough for Al Banks to
fleece him of $12,000 I paid him for the
business. I still owed Bill a few dollars for the
business when he returned. He took over
another old cycle shop he had competed with for
years, the Triumph dealer, who had more in
common with Bill than motorcycles.
It was Bill's old girlfriend who was now the widow
of the Triumph dealer. It was not easy to take
over a business previously owned by Bill—he
intimidated
anyone and every city official who ever
suggested he adapt to the city

building codes. I found this out after Bill left for Phoenix. The city decided to test
their building codes. "Don't you have a door in this place?" "Well you got in,
didn't you?" "You should have a regular walk-in door, not just an overhead
door. This is a business, isn't it?" "Besides, that's not why I am here." You
could tell he was a bureaucrat with the little black bow tie and McArthur
jacket. "You have to have a permit to put in a parking lot. You're not going
to run this place like Bill did? Now you are going to be cited for several
code violations and you'll get a notice from the city solicitor in a few days."
Well, it wasn't business as usual when I took over Bill's motorcycle shop, but
that's the way politics works. One person can break the laws for years and
then—wham—the new guy gets all the crap, so to speak.  My lawyer and the
city authorities finally resolved my building code violations.  Bill never did
become a competitive threat.

It was the dead of winter, when motorcycles were polished, not ridden.
Within hours of his return from Phoenix, Bill came directly to my motorcycle
shop for money. He barely had enough to buy gas for the trip home. "Where's

my money?" he said. "You were right, that son of a bitch got me good." But I
said, "Bill, I don't have any money! There's two feet of snow on the ground."
He said, "I don't have any place to stay, and I am broke. Al Banks ran off with
the whole $12,000 I gave him to invest." Bill's eyes looked old and teary, not like I
remembered him when he literally floated around the motorcycles tightening
and adjusting what seemed like ten screws or bolts simultaneously. He was
a racer in his day, and even though he limped when he walked, he seemed
to float effortlessly around the motorcycles in his crowded shop. He had old
coffee cans strategically placed, some with nuts and bolts, and some were
spittoons for his tobacco-chewing habit. Bill and I made a deal to clean up what I owed him as I relinquished a valve-facing machine from the inventory I originally purchased from him. Now that Bill's been dead for twenty years, I can count the departed motorcycle riders, not to suggest that Bill's or my business affected their demise, but I continue to ride. I felt sorry for Bill that day and until the day he died.   He seemed not to get a fair share from the standards we like to compare at the end of everyone's career or life. It seemed like a dreadful day again in the winter when I went to the funeral parlor. There was Bill. Everything

seemed to be the same in the room except the motorcycles were replaced
by baskets of flowers. It seemed like Bill was laid out on his workbench
instead of a casket. The faces were the same. You could hardly notice that
these were the same bodies I normally associated with gloves, boots, and
leather jackets. Their tone was low and childlike, not at all the image that
they wore daily. I was surprised to see an occasional tie. As I drove home, I
was considering how Bill measured up in this world. He died broke, worn
but adored. I considered the standard and eased my thinking by simply
saying, "I suppose it's better to die broke and worn than rich and alone."
He reminded me of the stuffed gorilla. Bill and the gorilla were certainly
dead and would do no harm, but even though the gorilla was stuffed and
moved about on wheels, it commanded great respect and even fear that
it could leap into life at any moment. I believe that all great people leave
this impression, but we don't stuff people.

Dare to be Great…

Always looking for a stepping stone to my fortune, as luck or unluck would have it, I met
Glen W. Turner… a cross between a southern

preacher and an escapee from a southern chain gang.  Not that Glen was a violent criminal, but a conman extraordinaire – capable of spinning a fantastic future in believing that everyone can accomplish anything they set their mind to.  Glen was the son of a share-cropper, dirt poor, exploited in his youth and plagued with a hair lip. He started a new company in Orlando, Florida – within the hype and public interest of Disney World's Epcot City – "Koscot" cosmetics.  The timing was right to pick off the remnants of the recent economic down turn of the late 60's - Semi would be mover and shaker types who missed the recent boat to wealth.   The entrance fee was $5000 – a nifty sum in 1970, but it entitled you to recruit distributors and split the money with Turner, Koscot.  The early days when the pyramid program was just starting had many entrants simply selling the franchise and no mind to the product, " Koscot Cosmetics". The products were by any standard very good and your $5000 entrance fee also provided you with $2500 worth of cosmetics.  It was your job then to hire door to door sales ladies to sell the lipstick and Glen's signature products containing mink oil.

But, the early days attracted the greedy, who only saw the big money in selling franchises. The scheme began to create some irritated franchisees and before long, the states attorney generals started to look into the issues… it was suggested that the pressure on the attorney generals was instigated by other more

established door to door cosmetic companies.
As the problems began to mount, Glen figured
that new franchisees needed to learn to sell and
build their self confidence. His new program
was called "Dare to be Great" which worked the
same way as the cosmetic company…the
program cost $5000 and a commission of $2500
was paid to the up-line sales person – the
balance was company profit less the week long
training and expenses in an Orlando motel. The
money making potential was too much to be
ignored by the "high roller" around Orlando, New
York, Pittsburgh or Cleveland. Yes, I fell for the
cosmetic franchise. Barbara started a "party
house" in the house I bought from Bill Black
behind the motorcycle shop. Actually, the selling
of the products was very good. The customers
were well satisfied and came back for more. It
seemed that all of our customers became beauty
advisers and all was moving along as planned.
It was the success of the actual product and the
enthusiasm of the sales people that caused the
fall of Koscot. It had simply been a great thorn in
the side of the "pink Cadillac" ladies. The
franchising method became a big issue with the
Attorney Generals and the publicity spilled over
into the products acceptability. The bad press
generated by the competition ranged from
causing skin cancer to stealing from poor old
grandmothers. Lesson - "your competition can
be well connected with the government" they
fund their political campaigns and contribute to
the universities. Yes, universities – here is

where products are authenticated when Dr. and Masters degreed professors who are paid hefty fees, by private companies, endorse products. It is a tangled web of locking in the market for those who know this lesson. It looked like the cosmetic side of the program would be short lived, and it was… but the Dare to be Great program continued, some making a handsome living and others, like myself, learning how to inspire people and generally live a "Dale Carnegie" life.

I have always looked at life like following a bell curved graph – along the ascending side and the descending side will be those blips which sometimes make or break you. I have always considered that success is winning 51% of the time – a home run is great but life's successes are determined by base hits, blips. Looking back on Glen Turner, even though he was a conman, I frankly believe he changed my life for the better. Success doesn't always go to the stronger or swifter man, but always to the man who thinks he can. It was only a year or so after the Turner blip that I found myself struggling to put a money making formula together – I was jumping up from the bottom of the barrel when an old friend who was a district manager for Fiat automobiles told me that Fiat might be able to use me as a district manager in another territory. I was given a trial job with Fiat to help a grossly over stocked dealer to move about 100 new one and two year old Fiat economy cars. The dealer was located about 40 miles from my home and each morning and evening I was treated to a one hour commute. I interpreted the offer by Fiat to see if I could handle a district manager position. It was not that they needed a district manager, I later discovered, it was that they needed a trouble shooter to go to all the dealers who were over stocked and couldn't move the troubled cars and work them out of their bloated inventories.

After two months I had setup some great promotions to draw attention to the Fiat cars…. an economy run with an invitation to some of the principle foreign brands, Honda, Nissan, Toyota, VW, etc. to participate. It was a great success, even though Fiat came in 2$^{nd}$. I was criticized by the dealer owner because we didn't win. I could have retaliated by saying," if your so smart why am I here to clean up your mess" – I explained to him that Avis rent a car always claimed to be number two – even when they were 1$^{st}$ - It would not have looked like we were impartial if we would have come in 1$^{st.}$ … Since we setup the entire event.

There is an under dog mentality we enjoy as Americans – it bestows energy and hope in a big way, just below deck. The old inventory started to move. I was praised for the sales success but I learned as soon as this dealer is back on his feet I could be moved on to another dealer about

150 miles from my home and repeat the experiment – that ended the blip.

Friends come out of the woodwork….

It was a similar situation that started a longer blip. It began a decade of getting my act together. If you are out of the house and moving about even a blind hog will find an acorn once and a while. My old friend Chuck in Bethesda, MD, from the motorcycle days, called me with his unusual excitement – "Suzuki Jeeps". "I'm the Northeast distributor." I paused about 30 seconds and tried to determine if he had been drinking. "Are you there", "Yes" I could hear his rapid breathing and then he told me the rest of the story. I said I'd really like to be the road rep and could start next week. I arrived in Bethesda, saw a little yellow Suzuki Jeep on the back of a Chevy heavy duty pickup truck  - it was too long to close the tail gate as it stuck out over the back of the truck… This was a little new to me but the exercise of driving the Zuki up to 8 ft ramps and into the pickup was just about the same as riding a motorcycle up a ramp into the back of a truck – I did it hundreds of time. Chuck gave me a nice all expense base salary and a hefty commission. I was surprised how easy it was to sell these little Zukies. It was only a few months on the road and the back orders became the sand in the grease. I oversold the supply and Chuck was beside himself not getting the merchandise to sell and support the cost of distribution.   We tried our best to pace the sales and take care of the dealer complaints but within six months we had to pull back and go to work on getting the supplies.   The problem came to my attention about the same time – Chuck was not purchasing the Zukies from Suzuki proper.  They were gray market imports from the Philippines and the Caribbean.  Suzuki in Japan was not ready to service the US market nor had they gotten Department of Transportation approval for the Zukies.  I followed Chuck's efforts for about 25 years thereafter as he continued to fight for the distribution rights – it left him exhausted and without ever having his day in court.

Energy Crisis 1972

I was reading through Automotive New after the rise and fall of Zuki – the situation looked grim indeed.  While looking through the ads and reading about the Oil embargo, I wondered how I could do something to help out or get involved. The previous two years had been kind to my bank account so I had the free time and financial support to investigate.   Like a blip on the bell curve of life I saw an ad looking for distributor of the Manful Fuel Booster… reading on I decided to telephone the company in Cleveland, yes, within two days I was on my way to Cleveland to meet Frank Manfuldi… inventor of the Fuel Booster.  It turned out to be a contradiction to *be judging* by its cover… Frank was not at all the engineering type I expected.  He was a line worker for GM into the 1960's, now retired and trying to market a product that had no market... at least not until the Oil embargo. Frank had rented a dingy 2nd floor factory space ten years previous and started to make a water ingestion system for cars and trucks. He had a great line and was able to entice about 90 investors into his company over the years. The Loraine and 28th St location near the rusting hub of Cleveland which looked relatively safe in the daylight but I never ventured there after work. Frank had arranged to meet me that first morning at a local diner breakfast spot in Parma. He was a quaint old guy with a sharp nose and bristly, but thinning hair – his Italian connections was everywhere on his face and his demeanor.

The Factory

Frank, after lunch, took me to his home to meet his family. They were just like the Italians I knew in Altoona, committed to family support and family pride. It was obvious as we drove into the Loraine area that this little old guy would first try to see if you were real and not a conman. He always said that he could tell in a few minutes if you were to be trusted. He liked to imagine that if you were turned upside down he could tell by the amount of money that fell out if you were a cheat... At this point I could see that his entire world was about to hit bottom but suddenly at a time when the top of the barrel was at its lowest point in his life he could jump out and make a big hit. Frank didn't realize how a unique and pivotal position he was in – the fuel crisis had only crossed his mind but didn't sink in. For me I could see a golden opportunity to sell this product. The advertising Frank had been running over the years was for installing dealers. It was clear to me that his factory and financial situation was not in a position to supply even one good dealer. In the past 10 years he had only sold about 200 units which sold for $169 each. He had been supporting the overhead on his little factory out of his own pocket and the money he had sucked out of his 90 or so investors. There were shelves of plastic parts and fasteners and about 40 power units (the most expensive part) available for assembly. I could see within our first five minute tour of the factory Frank was not going to be able to put this thing on the road unless he could raise some money.

I was invited to dinner at the Manfuldi home – a great Italian supper and good vibration. I simply told Frank before the dinner was over his plight. With tears in his eyes he finally understood that his product needed a professional to launch it – I told him that it had to done within the next 30 days or he would miss the boat. I left for home the next morning and as I entered the door Barbara said that Frank from Cleveland had called twice to speak with you. I had learned from past experiences the best way to have someone come your way was to back off and allow them to come your way... I did this instinctively – the next Monday morning I left at four AM to lay out a plan for the Fuel Booster at Frank's little factory in Cleveland. Frank was somewhat prepared by having some of his family members there to help. They agreed to a salary and full expense arrangement to begin as soon as the money would come in... Frank didn't realize my strategy... I was going to have a big stock holders meeting at the Ramada Inn in Parma in 10 days. The family dug out the stockholders list and I prepared an invitation to each for a grand meeting at the Ramada – with a complimentary buffet. The invitation was directed to the facts – it showed the current stock holders the fuel crisis implication of their company investment and now having patiently waited for a big payoff, it was time to cash in. The meeting was scheduled for six PM, all was ready; however, the stockholders were arriving hours early.

The Meeting:

Frank was not to have a speaking part in the meeting. I would conduct the entire affair with the intended purpose of having the stock holders buy more stock. Ah, experience... I remember conducting cosmetic seminars; dare to be great motivational meetings, all the necessary tools to motivate those stockholders. My strategy was to point out that they had already shown confidence in the product; they didn't need to be convinced that the product was useful – all that was needed was to load the gun. This time the target was right in front of them, the energy crisis. At about nine PM we had an additional commitment of slightly over $20,000. It was as if the energy gods had spoken to the crowd. Frank and his entire family began to see the light after a near death experience. The next problem was to hire several assemblers and get the key ingredients back in stock. There came into vision that most of the previous suppliers hadn't been paid for what they already supplied – I twisted some arms and got the credit thing resolved by paying up front before delivery. These minor obstacles took a week out of my progress but the energy crisis continued to plague America. I went to Automotive News in Detroit and installed a fuel booster on one of the staff's vehicles who promised to write a report within two weeks – it was a very hot topic in the automotive industry, especially for the market the product... the desperate car dealers, with these hugh inventories of gas guzzlers, could buy one for each car and put them on as any other accessory. BINGO – the editorial report, even though cautious in it findings, lit off a wave of buying by the car dealers. We had order for over a 1000 units by the end of the 1st month – Frank was going crazy trying to get help assembling and packaging the Boosters. The interesting part of the sales message was not that the Booster was an honest fuel saver; it was used as an incentive to soften the fears of new car buyers. The dealers really didn't care if it actually reduced fuel consumption as long as the consumer translated the message in a way that resulted in selling more cars.

My experience with automobiles and motorcycles, my college chemistry and physics, and my early experiences at home worked well with understanding the principles of fuel economy. The Second World War introduced a similar device related to using water injection to improve various conditions in military aircraft engines. There was a company, also in Cleveland that later was sold to TRW, a major supplier of aircraft items, that produced the aircraft version of the fuel booster. Could it have been the model for Frank – that question was never resolved... anyway the two products functioned in a similar way but not to the advantage of Frank's design. Frank's booster simply created partially vaporized water that could be inhaled by the engine when operated under high manifold vacuum. At the time of his development, auto engines were producing forward motion with higher crankshaft revolutions per mile than the current crop of new gas guzzlers. Yes, Frank's booster did perform in these older cars because the cruising speeds used higher manifold vacuum – it was the vacuum that inhaled the moist air into the engine.

The chemistry or science that supports the water theory in engines has never really been settled however, I will give you my opinion. It is conceivable that the moist air becomes disassociated and the water molecules break up into Hydrogen and Oxygen and in a re-combining at the point of combustion act as a fuel – reducing the amount of fuel to move the vehicle. Well, that was one of the messages – another is that the moisture when subjected to the intense heat of combustion turns to steam and occupies more volume and pressure on the pistons. That being said I decided to look at the use of water in the WWII aircraft – here as a better answer to the question – the water was injected only at take-off when full power was needed. The fuel available was not always of a high anti-knock (hi octane) quality so water was injected to slow the flame propagation in the cylinders. The water injection actually interfered with the combustion process therefore high compression ratios could be used without damage to the engine. Note, under full power an engine is operating at its lowest manifold vacuum.

Two months into the Booster game I began to have the time to work on improving the booster – that is, making the booster work better in the newer cars which operated on low manifold vacuum. The EPA had changed the Detroit style of engine use by pushing the use of Catalytic converters to reduce emissions. The old engines didn't respond well to the EPA's emissions requirements. The engines were forced to turn slower at cruising speeds so the emissions per mile could be reduced. That meant Frank's booster would be compromised further even if it did works somewhat in the older cars. Frank never took criticism well and he just didn't have the background or temperament to understand my push for a redesign. After ninety days sales began to level off but new interest from Europe kept the product alive and quite well at this point. Renault shipped a complete vehicle over from France. The engineer and I installed the booster and drove around the Cleveland beltways for two days interpreting the results on several pre-installed engine monitoring devices – results were dismal. The engineer said that my redesign would obviously improve the performance and offered to re-evaluate when it was ready. It never happened – Frank flew to Italy and became involved with some international venture that drained all the profits for the Cleveland operation – My nearly a year in Cleveland established me, and I was accepted into the SAE (Society of Automobile Engineers).

While I was in Cleveland I had a few visits with an old friend from the motorcycle days, Tom Lester, he was one of the key figures in everything automotive. Tom owned a die-casting plant that had captured virtually every Detroit auto manufactures business – parts for fuel systems, design services and basically every American car was hostage to Tom's Lester Industries. Was he wealthy? You bet. A billionaire in the 1960s was truly a rare financial entity. Tom's real love was the historic record of the automobile industry. In conjunction with his other business he had purchased the molds from Goodyear and Firestone for every size tire ever created... set up a tire company which specialized in these rare tires. His other fascination was restoration and collecting vintage automobiles. If he couldn't find one for his collection he would build it – I mean completely - from blue prints to fabrication of the frame and body to the casting and forging the drive train. Actually, Tom didn't figure into my vision because he would try to turn my every social visit into an employment opportunity. I could see how he commanded his closest staff, who were paid more than their worth, into being lap dogs and go-for's to his slightest request. I could understand the message of Jesus "Man doesn't live by bread alone". Well, after a visit to Tom's for another lunch employment offer, I stopped at Central Cadillac, while speaking with the service manager we were disturbed by a loud crashing sound and workers scurrying around the back of the repair shop. As the conversation was abruptly severed I wondered back to the source of the confusion. There it was a new Cadillac with the hood crushed in like a broken beak – the new equipment intended to wash cars was the culprit. A very large and heavy brush had fallen on the Caddy and crumpled the hood. As I observed the reactions of a few of the workers I could tell that they were just installing the machine and it was obvious they were being held responsible to the damage to the new car. I took a look for myself and could see that the chain that controlled the guilty brush had broken. There was one fellow, who by his dress and demeanor, was a wash machine company official. The conversations and directives were taking aim at responsibility. I heard the boss say he would contact the factory and have a new chain sent up overnight. Without excusing myself I offered my two cents worth, "You can get that chain size just down the street", His name was, Harry and I caught his attention like a dog spotting a cat, " That's #50 motorcycle chain, we can get right down the street at the Harley Davidson dealer". Harry Smith was the son-in-law of one of the founders of the Rivens Chester Car Wash Co. Over dinner that evening Harry couldn't express his gratitude enough that I was able to salvage the sale of the new car wash machine. By the time dessert was served Harry offered me a chance to be a sales rep for the company. I had the technical background and knew the car dealer language like a mission statement of a politician. The deal was really just to my liking – they would send me inquiries from their sales campaigns and I would go and sell the washers – I was good with the dealers as I always said I would be there for installation to make certain everything went well, and collect the final check.  I liked to work this way, I paid my own expenses, but collected a big commission.  I also controlled my personal life by being able to work when I wanted to and in my own way.   I had to say good bye to Frank and his greed focused ambition.  I left Cleveland a week later and turned the company operation over to one of the major stockholders.

I can still see the only real friends I made in Cleveland – five dogs, mutts… that timed their unsupervised morning walk about 8:30 AM to arrive near the entrance of the Booster factory. One day I had a left- over sandwich from the night before.  I gave each a piece of the sandwich and they went on their way.  The next morning I arrived early, I could see the five mutts waiting to cross the fast traffic area of Loraine. These fellows were street savvy; the leader, a bull dog mix with only one eye was the traffic checker… when it was clear, they all followed. If I was late, they were waiting for their snack; if I was early, I always waited for them to cross Loraine alive.  I hope that someone else got acquainted with them after I left.  I missed them at first, but like all other things in life, time has a way of healing.

It wasn't long before several other car and truck wash companies took notice of my progress at their expense.  I had offers to move up and above my present place in the industry and I finally did. I could see that the real opportunities were in the manufacturing business but it took me another decade to find the right slot for me. In the meantime I began to have products private labeled that I could fit into my car wash business… steam cleaners, truck accessories and chemicals. I found myself traveling most of the eastern United States supervising and developing processes for cleaning trucks, busses and cars, like Trailways, US Postal Service and UPS. I always appreciated one of UPS's internal slogans… all we have to offer is "clean trucks and good service". I thought of myself as offering more than clean trucks and good service, I was getting tired of the pace. It was keeping me too busy. The bean counters were always looking for ways to better the bottom line. One of the major problems of the transportation industry was the rust and corrosion to their rolling stock. Aside from looking good to the owners they were trying to make their vehicles last longer. Somewhere along the way this became a seed planted for the future.

While things were going great with the wash industry there was the nagging effects of traveling – so much time was consumed just to make your calls; it took away from your hobbies and personal life. As I look back I had many unrelated interests during those years – I liked my watch hobby, motorcycles, gun, dogs and most of all my family. The girls were starting to drive and I wanted to be at home more often. My daughter, Monica had insight, she could see trends. Monica saw a trend in the 1980's as a result of high energy prices. The kerosene heater became the new Honda phenomena – a clever device that was used to heat most of the homes in Japan. Now they began to appear in the USA – so we opened a store… just for these heaters. I knew that they would be big sellers for about three years and I was right – we sold thousands of them, retail and mail order. It was during this time that I began to think about the seed I had planted for the future. It came to me as I remembered my Penn State chemistry professor telling about using electric current to reduce the rusting of ocean going vessels. I could see that the automobile industry had been changing and instead of turning cars over after six years into scrap, people were keeping their cars longer and rust was becoming a vicious adversary to long term ownership. The message kept kicking me for more than a year and I began to dig deeper into the theory and application of electric currents and if they could be used to protect cars and trucks. I declined more involvement in the car wash area so I to decided to sellout the private label business and stay closer to home. We had some really spectacular years in the small heating device business good enough to purchase a commercial building and look like everyone else. The anti-rust concept had gripped my thinking for months. I came up with a crude product which had never been applied to the auto industry…

What shall we call it?

This time around I tried a descriptive name…it was actually not what the anti-rust product did but how clever the description developed attention. Even though it did not bust-up already rusted metal parts, the "RustBuster" hit the mark in the automotive circles. The actual principle was similar to the rust reducing concept my chemistry professor described which was used on ocean vessels. I didn't have a facility to produce the RustBuster so I had to contract the work out. The 1$^{st}$ obstacle was the quantity required by the most professional and reliable firms – I couldn't meet their requirement of 100,000 pieces. I scaled down my vision of working only with the most reliable suppliers scratching them off the list and finally realizing that I would have to go to the fly-by night under capitalized assemblers – at least I believed that if I kept my eye on them I could keep them honest. Well, there is an old saying, "if you want it done right do it yourself".

I will spare you the gory details of lost time, money and opportunity. I could simply say that I entered into two very costly contracts with very unscrupulous persons. Their intent was to steal the idea and my money or both. I learned that Canadian law has an element that is absent in

USA law – if you want to sue you must pay up
front to take action… I did and I won.  In the USA
I had to sue and found that my opponent using
the convolution of our laws caused me to lose
money.  Those actions brought me to the
realization that I had to become the
manufacturer.  It was tough putting the product
together and trying to protect the concept from
infringers.  I found that our trademark, copyright
and patent laws are only useful to big boys,
those who already have the market, the
universities and the various governments in their
pocket.  I should have stopped running after this
ambitions project after 18 months of fighting just
to get it off the ground, but the limited advertising
I did created a demand that was too tantalizing
not to
go after.

It was after one big ad in Popular Mechanics
magazine that I learned that just like my dad told
me, "you can't fight city hall".  I was only sixteen
when I nearly got hit by a Street Car, dad said if
they run into you it will be your fault – The city
will sue you for the damage they caused.  That
might be a poor example but it relates the power
that big companies have over the little guy.  My
patent and trademark attorney told me that the
name RustBuster was being opposed by the
Black & Decker Corp. as being confusing with
their product, the DustBuster.  A few weeks of
back and forth telling Black & Decker that I
would suffer serious lose if I had to abandon the

name; they offered my attorney $5000 if I would abandon the name.   My attorney made a counter offer of higher value and told me that Black & Decker was considering making the offer a bit sweeter.  Weeks went by without any progress in the matter.  I had already received several calls about my revolutionary product so I was accustomed to giving telephone interviews. Then a reporter from a Baltimore newspaper was interviewing me about the RustBuster.  The reporter asked me if the name really described the products' value.  He said it sounded like DustBuster, I said, in fact Black&Decker thought that also.  The reporter went on and so did I – at the end of the interview the reporter ask me if I changed the name wouldn't that cause you serious financial loss?  I replied that I had already decided on another name, one that was more descriptive and useful, so the loss would be minimal.  He said what is the new name?  I said, as if shouted with the help of a shofar, "RustEvader".

Two days later my attorney called and said that Black&Decker withdrew their offer and have counter sued me to abandon the name RustBuster – because of the article in the Baltimore newspaper.  It seems that the big guy tricked me and had a powerful newspaper in their pocket to do the dirty work.

RustEvader finally became a registered trademark, and several minor patents were about to issue. There was a very simple patent already issued that laid out a scheme to work against rust on automobiles. It was owned by a Professor at MIT, an employee of Texas Instrument. The Professor was very protective of his patent and of the science that were not covered in his patent. If fact he had never produced a working product that appeared in print or was subject to review. We had no direct communication but that was short lived. When RustEvader started to get international interest, I got a call from a Canadian who wanted to get in on the opportunity – he said he could smell the money. Canada is plagued by salt encrusted roadways, a nasty winter climate seven months out of the year, cars and trucks simply fall apart from corrosion. It started off with the Canadian buying a few of my RustEvaders and within three months he approached me with a plan to be the exclusive Evader man in Canada. I was still having trouble meeting demand and told him that I couldn't manage his requirement. A few months later the Canadian said he had formed a company with investors and wanted to purchase a license to build the product in Canada. I could even take advantage of the extra production for my other markets. I had an uncomfortable feeling that I was being sucked into a situation where my control would be compromised. I managed to rationalize my feelings and tried to sell myself on the advantages and not the potential pitfalls. A deal was struck allowing the Canadian to assemble and distribute the

Evaders only in Canada. I withheld a critical part that he was not allowed to produce, the anodes, I thought that would keep him honest.

The Canadian's real motivation was to start an investment scam. He formed a company and advertised for investors. The claims made for the Evader were down-right exaggerated and misleading. The company grew rapidly now heavily invested with cash. They began to advertise the product to the public with the same exuberance they attracted investors. Mr. MIT caught wind of the advertising placed by the Canadian and went to Canadian Consumer Affairs with a scalding rebuttal of the claims being made for the Evader. This now became a hot potato in the United States as well. We had kept our advertising message conservative, and within reasonable bounds. There was a cooling off period with the Canadian who withdrew his aggressive promotions and for about a year the landscape began to quiet.

The Canadian who had to justify his investment scam came to me and offered one million dollars to buy me out. I frankly thought it a good idea. I had been bombarded by problems since conceiving the Evader. When it came time to make the exchange the Canadian Gov. stepped in and closed down the stock scheme. The Canadian was basically put out of business. The complications surrounding the distribution were overwhelming. Being the designer, the factory steward, and Mr. Evader everything - had to stop. My family, accountant, attorneys and friends all advised, "Get some help". One of our dealers had some marketing people in Pittsburgh that came in to look over the situation. I had just purchased a bigger facility with plenty of room to grow. The marketing people put together a plan that looked first class and reasonable. The three formed a new a marketing company. Call it Marketing Co. for short. Their attorneys worked an agreement that tightly bound us all together. Now some of the pressure was off my shoulders since they were now responsible for sales… and that is how they got paid – a big percentage.

A coin has two sides:

Just when you think you can relax, the winds of change work their magic. Barbara, the girls and I have lived in the family section of rural PA for decades only to be told that all three of our properties were being taken under eminent domain to build a new school. There were other neighbors involved but no amount of legal ease or disease could change the public's demand for our property. I found myself in the midst of looking for new housing for my entire family and trying to run the Evader business. The Evader business now was about 40 employees strong. I decided to retire from active involvement, retain the chair of chairman of the board and allow the three marketing guys to become President, and two vice presidents. I had given up literally all the control of the company image. The RustEvader Corp did well selling the product in about 10 different countries and establishing a major presence in the automotive aftermarket. The RustEvader was sellable because of the way it was sold. It s was sold in the traditional way of adding it to all the new cars a dealer would inventory. It was automatically packed on to the retail price. The dealers loved the Evader's easy of installation, the piggy back waxes and fabric conditioners that went with it. The dealers were throwing out the spray rust proofing systems they had used for decades and now only had to deal with a clean environmentally friendly little black box. The dealers had eliminated one of the problems that the spray on systems caused – some customers simply didn't believe in the spray-on products and many were suspicious, and rightly so, that they in fact supported rust and corrosion. But once the spray on tar was on the car… you couldn't take it off. Sales were so good that the biggest dealers in the Ohio rust belt were installing 500 to 700 units a month each.

Now let's follow the money… The Evader was now taking substantial business from a Detroit based spray-on coating industry rust proofer. The industry was really quite huge perhaps as much as several hundred million dollars a year. These companies employed many hundreds of workers and these companies had become a depository for waste oil and pollutant chemicals which were not fit to be pumped into a land fill. They were blended and sprayed on as many new cars as possible. You can see where this is going… someone wins, someone loses. The spray industry had a following in the political arena with their support of favored Detroit politicians. The tar industry also had to support the politicians against the environmental side of their waste products… remember what my Chemistry Prof said – "find out what is being thrown away and find a way to sell it" – well that's exactly what was going on.

I managed to find a 60 acre piece of undeveloped land in the rural area my family had enjoyed for years. Undeveloped turned out to be nearly impossible to develop. Lanes had to be bull dozed in, wells had to be drilled, construction sheds built and it had to be done quickly as our time to vacate the condemned houses had nearly expired. I was also in a vicious fight to get approval for sand mounds and reduced restriction for wetlands… for a year my association with RustEvader was left to the genius of the marketing and company officials. Little did I know that they were in a serious struggle with the spray on rust proofers – in an effort to quiet the rust proofer from continuing their negative advertising about the Evader – our company president instituted a law suit against them. He claimed unfair competition, malicious and derogatory statements. Well, now I was needed to make some sense of the situation because I had to develop a defense for RustEvader as a viable product, therefore forcing the detractors to cease and desist their unfounded comments.

A funny thing happened on the way to the Moon...

My accountant also entered the picture and what he said was a total shock... Your officers are stealing you blind. This would take another book to retell. I was forced to fire the President, and take over the President's position and the headaches he had caused. The vice presidents were only slightly tainted. Our attorneys went through months of depositions, expert testimony and money – finally, the rust proofers were found to owe RustEvader nearly $200,000. Sounds like we should be celebrating – not so fast... Remember, I stated that the rust proofers were well connected in the political arena – they were. They instigated, with the help of their political friends, an inquiry by the Federal Trade Commission. The inquiry required RustEvader to appear in the FTC regional office in Cleveland along with my attorney and a truck load of company documents. The FTC already had the entire case history and documents from the proceedings with the rust proofing settlement. The FTC instantly pointed out that we couldn't support our advertising claims. The FTC said that our testing and independent laboratory tests were inadequate and in fact anecdotal. The following year was a combination of defending ourselves against the unlawful dismissal of the company president and negotiating a settlement with the FTC. Word spread that the FTC was going to enjoin the auto dealers in their investigation – RustEvader was finished, no car dealer wanted involved, they stopped selling the RustEvader system – essentially putting us out of business.

Time marches on:

It was time to move to our new homes and we had to transport several lifetimes of stuff accumulated over the years. My vintage watch collection was subject to 'Barbara's comment, "What are you going to do with all those watches"? I had been a watch hobbyist since I was a teenager. The internet had become a new marketing tool which was especially attractive to object collectors and watch collectors in particular. I had been a member of the National Association of Watch Collectors and bought, sold and traded watches at their regular shows around the country. The internet opened a new and fast marketing avenue. I moved all the watch collection and associated stuff to our new home in the mountains and set up to start selling my collection rather than trying to fit it into our new house. Within a year my collection had become completely thinned out. I continued to practice my old habit of searching for old watches – and it soon became more and more difficult to find them. The popularity of the internet with the watch collectors changed the collectors' landscape – the internet had become the new marketplace. Mechanical watches (those without batteries) had suddenly become the obsession of those interested in watches. With old mechanical watches becoming very scarce, I decided that new mechanical watches would be my next step in the collector market.

Collectors highly valued limited production and numbered timepieces. So after many months of searching small manufacturers of Swiss watches I had my own design fabricated. It was a see-through mechanical watch, known in the industry as a skeleton watch. It was a handsome men's wrist watch with a refined 17 jewel movement – it was an instant success.


Moving to a new home, fighting with ex-employees, wrestling with the Federal Trade Commission, caring for my aging mother, playing the church organ, and taking the exhausting task of developing a large parcel of land… left me breathless. I was never ready to quit, I simply had learned that if you have a tooth ache get it fixed or get it out.

I had learned in the past and was coached by my dad - you must learn to retreat and live to fight another day. When dealing with Bureaucrats it's best to allow them to push you around, (one of the worlds great boxers called it the rope-a-dope) if you resist these crat's they become energized and thrive on ways to make your life miserable. When a government agency starts an action against you – you have already lost. They have resources to engage you with, that the individual cannot hope to rebut because of the high financial cost of doing so. They will have already collected an entire plan to put into action before the first words are spoken. The Bureaucrats do not like to be challenged but they do have a human side… they are basically lazy and when they are winning they are weak and will settle claims against you quickly and painlessly, winning is more important then the content of settlement. Bureaucrats use their great power to ride roughshod over popular issues and people. You become a rung in their ladder to more powerful government positions. The attorney general of one of our great states was particularly focusing on making aftermarket auto accessories, including rust resistant products, added to the new car prices banned and illegal. It never became law but the publicity around his actions in the media and false saber rattling scared the car dealers from doing it and educated the public as to how they were being screwed… speaking of screwed, it was only a few years later that this same attorney general found himself wrapped up in a sex scandal that forced him from office – but, he is now a TV show pundit spewing the virtues of liberalism. You can't fight city hall and the media – and I didn't I, simply had to take the medicine to cure the FTC's indigestion of RustEvader.

Retreat to fight another Day…

The bottom line was that RustEvader simply went out of existence because the auto dealers were afraid to sell it. I personally owned the building and manufacturing facilities. I began to look for a way of using the left over parts. Most of the items were electronic and could be modified for some other purpose. I read an article in National Geographic's showing the use of electric current to draw moisture in the soil near the leaning tower of Pisa. The concept lingered in my mind for a while and then it hit me – this might be a way to increase crop growth if the electric current could be used to draw moisture to the roots of plants. I set up an experiment in a tomato patch, one row of electronic induced moisture and a row without the electronic help. The system worked, the electronic row gave better, bigger and faster growing tomatoes. There was another ideal that I thought had merit – putting an electric current into a fish tank and see if fish are attracted by the current – they are!

In the years leading up to the demise of RustEvader, I had patented automotive sparkplug electrode configurations, a magnetic attachment to oil filters and a polytetraflorethelene dry lubricant additive for engine oil. These patents have been left to expire. I simply didn't find the pleasure in trying to launch new products and cope with the potential headaches that are associated with paradigm shifts in the marketplace. It was during these years that the long siege of my mother came to an end. I was ready to make a change and Barbara and I did... we sold everything and moved to Arizona.

It only took a few weeks for us to adjust to Arizona. Life started over for us. We had left the past behind. My watch business had grown and it supported us modestly as we entered our retirement years. I have looked back thinking that perhaps I should have concentrated on watches right out of high school. Then I think about the vast memorable experiences with my daughters, our family solidarity, our wonderful dogs and animal friends – success isn't easy. Success is the vision you have painted from memory. I wouldn't change a thing. The rewards have been greater than wealth. After our five year rehab in Arizona we were ready to return to Pennsylvania and we settled in the town where my great grand father was born and where my wife grew up – home is sweet.

Life is caught in the grasp of fate's own choosing....

Well, it's New Year's Day again. We have had
snow since November 9th. First
it was a massive two-foot accumulation sprinkled
with a minor blizzard and
a two-day thaw just before Christmas. For those
two short days of brilliant
sunshine and warmer temperatures, it seemed
as though nothing had changed.
It was October again, but just as quickly as the
snow had melted, Mother
Nature slapped us silly on Christmas Day with
continued flaking and pelted
us with frozen particles from heaven. I haven't
decided whether New Year's
Day is a good time for reflection or anticipation.
Our news media continued
to pound on past miseries and human failures. I
prefer to think of New Year's
Day as a possible one small step that mankind
might try to erase his failures
and set a course toward tranquility and peace.
The lessons of fifty years ago have been either
forgotten or simply cast into the corners of
history. The United States is entering into a new
conflict.  Our politicians are telling us that we are
really not going to war just keeping us together.
Haven't we practiced that exercise before?

I foresee a Constitutional middle "C" meltdown

America is nearing the midpoint in man's search
for a better way of life.

The Boston Tea Party (BTP) was proverbially the last straw in framing our Constitution.  The Declaration of Independence, the preamble of man's best work to date, has endured to this day. We must never forget the brave acts of our forefathers—braving oceans in ships that by today's standard would not be safe to cross Boston Harbor.  The BTP is acknowledged not as a simple act that changed everything, but as a point of no return  in fighting for individual and collective rights.  Self-governed free men are not slaves to the greed of an irresponsible monarchy. Empires, with purposes contrary to man's best interest, have fallen into history. The manipulation of religion and laws, to support bondage, will never succeed.  The BTP proved that free men could and would muster the courage to resist the amoral godless principles that angered men's souls at the apex of any dark age.  Perhaps America is facing a new dark age of complicated rules and an obsession to cut ourselves off from God and the truth that has made us great. On guard, never forget the BTP. It should be your daily reminder that freedom is constantly being attacked. I relate this concept with this parallel: when staring at a Picasso painting, I

get the impression that he didn't, and perhaps no mortal could convey the
deepest human feelings in words. So he painted them and the meaning comes through. Our world is now straining to find words but we have no Picasso counterpart to express our plight.

Nature reminds us in subtle ways that freedom and independence are just a survival mechanism.  We have a flock of crows living near our house and they patiently wait for leftover bread or other snacks. I have become a distant and cautious part of those crows' lives. There is also a mean old hawk that lives in the area nesting somewhere in the tall oaks. Perhaps the crows have borrowed their battle tactics from Shakespeare's, Julius Caesar, "Sound and fury signifying nothing." Last summer, I stole a few moments to investigate a scrimmage taking place a few hundred feet above our power line. The hawk was diving and weaving with three and sometimes as many as six crows attempting to peck his tail feathers and render him flightless. This battle went on as long as I could take it. My neck began to pain from my unnatural posture so I withdrew from the observation, rubbing my neck and thinking that they may have been duplicating a real-life First World War dog fight somewhere over the Rhine River.

A few months later, just as spring had awakened the leaves, I was driving in

our lane with the window open looking for more signs of spring, when I saw a
couple of turkey vultures stumbling over logs and stones in a hot pursuit of a
wounded crow. I instinctively stopped the jeep and leaped over the edge of the
roadway to try to get a better look at what nature was trying to accomplish. My
commotion scared off the turkey vultures and the wounded crow continued
to struggle helplessly to avoid me. I suppose he thought me to be the mother
of all turkey vultures. I was able to pick the crow up, which was a remarkable
large bird but very light, with his eyes placed in such a way that it was virtually
impossible to see both eyes at one time. By looking at just one eye, I could
tell that this bird was plenty scared. I held him for a few seconds, collecting
my thoughts as to what I was going to do now that I had him. I figured he
would be dead meat for sure if I just put him back down on the ground. His
right wing was giving him some signal not to move, so I was careful not to
move it abruptly as I folded it gently back against its shiny black body. The
sunlight coming through the new leaves caused his feathers to glow rainbow
like oil on water. I held him for about a minute without moving much and

tried to soothe his psyche. As I walked back up the hill, I began to analyze
what I could do with this crow. I remember a few years earlier attempting to
nurse a few baby rabbits and they keeled over one right after the other in two
days, so I thought I'd put him in a pile of brush to mend for a few days on
his own. I carefully stacked walking stick size branches over and around some
melon size rocks I used to construct Mr. Crow's temporary hospital. I
carefully held him down with one hand using the other to put the finishing
touches on his lair. I was careful not to allow the dogs to follow me back
to the crow. I had some bread and some pieces of yesterday's roast which I
carefully placed within pecking distance. It was beginning to get dark by this
time, so I added a few more branches and was satisfied that, short of an act
of Congress, Mr. Crow would be safe at least for a couple of days. I suppose
man's actions tend to emulate nature. I felt good about being a peacekeeper.
It's part of what makes me tick. I feel compelled going about doing good
works for nature. Perhaps this is the motivation for peacekeeping.

We have just had another casualty. The television provides us with

vivid examples. Here we are again. It could be North Korea, the Battle of
some new Bulge with the soldiers fighting, not only with the enemy, but with Mother Nature. The TV shows us them building a pontoon bridge across a little river. You know the kind you've seen great painters use to express tranquility and peace. The painters were able to capture the best the river had to offer, a pleasant summer setting, children playing near the line of the shore, no cold and no despair. Yet our TV screen lets us know that this is a dreadful event and no man is really at peace. As peacekeepers, we will be marked in history as the country that goes about doing other peoples business, uninhibited by judgment, becoming hated by both sides.

There are big wars and little wars.

It's the human condition and the participants from a mugger to a massive government initiative. All contain the same ingredients: economic greed, dominance, and self-elevation. Political propaganda has adopted Einstein's principle of relativity. The relationship of energy to mass in Einstein's formula is dictated by the speed of the system whereas energy and mass are one and the same depending upon speed. Purposeful propaganda is created by the speed at which politicians abandon fact and truth. The distortion is created by the speed of glazing over the pertinent issues. You've heard the term, sound bites. These are shortened versions of the truth and neglected portions of the facts. Our gray matter is peppered with sound bites from all sources. Conflict is the world's way of tempering the spirit of mankind.  It is the first resort to survival.  Much is spoken about solving issues in a non-combative compromise, but instinct presses the easy button.  The individual is totally incapable of fully understanding the governmental system around him. Political institutions do not have a central nervous system or brain, which controls the rationale of their actions. It's not a tug-of-war between two horses, but a grand circle of thousands hitched to a central point that undulates like a jellyfish bobbing helplessly along the shore of the constitution.

.


I have always been impressed by the staggering scope of insignificance that a
drop of water might have on a river or a grain of sand in a desert. The intense
emotional feelings of my "middle C meltdown" was totally encapsulated in
me. The significance of scale in my internal being was grossly disproportionate.
I had suddenly become the desert or the river. The thoughts and reactions of
Mrs. Glover can only be represented as grains of sand or droplets of water.
Those reactions in reality meant nothing in my life and its future if I allowed

it. I didn't. This dreamy recall substantiates how your early childhood will
effect the rest of your life. Those high or low points will haunt you, direct you,
and give your decisions balanced or perhaps unbalanced rationale.

Chicken  & Canine  - middle "C" meltdown

Stray dogs have been my weakness. I attracted dogs. Do I smell good to them?
Do our eyes mesh? What's the magic here? I call it ESdogP. Out of necessity,
being an only child in a remote community, I cultivated this interaction.
My first family dog, a little white mixed Westie kind of chap, introduced
me to ESdogP. Babe was known to love canned peas. He was about five
years older than me and must have been very forgiving, as I only recall his
friendly nature. I suppose the canned peas were responsible for his demise.
He would beg and beg for them and we fed him until he would moan and
groan in either ecstasy or agony. It was a game. He would paw in the shelf
under the sink, knocking out a few canned vegetables, hoping we would get
the message and get his peas. He couldn't read the labels, but I am sure he
must have recognized the pictures on the cans. If a can of corn rolled out,

it was by accident. Like a four-legged Babe
Ruth, he would fetch peas with
an uncanny accuracy. At mealtime, especially
weekends, chicken would be
roasted; peas were the alternate choice for any
dinner vegetable. Babe waited
impatiently before dinner was served. Mother
always fed him just before the
family sat down. Babe would get the same
selection, but he would eat the
peas first and beg for more even with a few
pieces of chicken in his bowl.
Potatoes were not the alternate choice; they
were part of every meal—fried,
boiled, or mashed. Corn, canned corn, was the
alternate choice and served
in rotation every other Sunday. On alternate
Sundays, corn Sundays, Babe
would get his usual rations with corn instead of
peas. He would meticulously
separate the corn from the mashed potatoes,
never allowing one single grain
of corn to be swallowed. Babe's end did not
come easily or quickly like our
Sunday chickens that lost their heads on
Grandma's stump.

Our little valley or gap in the mountains had the
world famous Parks Poultry Farm. I was almost
a part of the Parks family; this close association
grew out of my grandparents' friendship with Joe
Parks, the inventor of the pure white chicken.
His son Bob, in his later years, kept a small flock

of wild ducks and a few geese in his pond. When the winter weather turned severe, I would take on the feeding of these poor captives. They had been bread-fed over the years losing their incentive to fly south with Bob for the winter. I suppose this is a parallel to our human condition—when government takes care of your every need, you lose incentive. Most families had their own chickens for eggs and meat. I was appointed to feed chickens and gather the eggs from our backyard barn. Chicken feeding was a challenge year round. In the summer I had to fight the black snakes for eggs and on cold winter mornings, the chickens were fed a ground dried vegetable mixed with hot water. The smell of that mixture tightened my esophagus forcing sour juices to swirl about the back of my throat. Today, when I feed my dogs, I mix some fresh burger with their packaged food. If the temperature during the mixing is too warm, I will begin to get that old gag reflex from the smell. I have always treated my dogs too well, giving them just about anything that smelled good to them. I suppose the peas might have contributed to Babe's slow choking, gasping, back porch end, not by a single can of peas, but rather like a smoker's accumulated consumption. I can't think now as to how I felt about this experience. I suppose the whacking of the chickens that graced our dinner table probably cushioned the blow, for me at least.

There is a technique, not a science, to killing
chickens. Grandma Annie had a
stump, about the size of a five-gallon can, flat on
the top with two large nails
hammered into the middle of the stump. The
nails were about two inches apart
and extended skyward about three inches high.
It could be described as a radial
crucifix. Chicken behavior is the same no matter
whether you are feeding them or
attempting to catch them. Chickens are
programmed not to get any closer than
a ten-foot pole to humans. There is no tricking a
chicken. They must be outrun.
Overtaking a chicken can cause you to stumble,
fall, get all dirty and muddy, and
look feebly inept, but using a shrinking
enclosure—that's the answer. I developed
this technique to save my dignity. I later learned
that I had not invented the wheel, just applied a
little ingenuity. Grandma had retained the lost
and sacred art of catching chickens… staring
them in the eyes until they would lay on their
side so she could grasp them by the two legs,
carry them over to the stump, and place their
heads between the two nails. Then with a swift
slash of the hatchet, remove their heads. The
next phase is very gruesome. She would let go
of the headless chicken spurting blood, and they
would run about and fall over dead.

As I recall, Dad was not a hunter, he was kind in
a chicken hearted way.  Dad's firsthand suffering

at home put him at the bottom of the pecking order. He remarked to me that his mother forced him to kill a chicken, his pet chicken. My dad's mother was not the favored grandmother of this writer; rather it was my mother's mother to whom I grew closer and closer throughout life. Dad's chicken killing, his chicken-hearted experience, was an expression of his true and high regard for life, even chicken life. He would recant the experience with the solemnity of a Palm Sunday pastor. He had made a friend of his victim. I have forgotten if he had a name for the pet, but it matters not here and now as he told about allowing the chicken to peck about for one more blade of grass before the execution. I perceived a strong resentment with Dad's mother's side of the family. That resentment was connected to a complex mix of circumstances resulting in unimagined poverty, shared by many during the Great Depression. Having been moved by it all I watched the poultry farm hang hundreds of chickens by the feet. I can still hear their screams for help as old Mr. Person would march along the killing line of hung chickens and cut their throats. Dutch, a sort of mix Boston terrier was coming to an end. Dutch was suffering and needed to be put down. I took her to the veterinarian, and even though I had been carrying her about for a few days, Dutch jumped from the car and began that dog ritual of smelling about the vet's grounds. As I tugged on the leash, it hit me how my dad felt about his pet chicken, allowing it to peck about one last time.

Now his words spilled over into my tearing eyes as I watched Dutch smell one last blade of grass. There were others on four legs that twisted my throat, which is one of my life's unmatched agonies. I was reviewing my old photos for this presentation and came across a picture of Andy, my Irish setter - what a majestic dog, true to his Irish nature he was an independent thinker and mastered by no man.

Now, I have a new foundling lying by my side...

As I write these notes he deserves a mention, not that so many other of my four-legged buddies are eclipsed, but Eighty was the most recent and challenging acquisition. Arizona gave me my one grand breakaway. I lived there for nearly five years, west of Phoenix. I had envisioned living in the Wild West before I reached my teens. I claimed Arizona for my home; however, there is no freedom from the past. An old stagecoach line, now blacktopped, runs from Wickenburg to Prescott. Route 89 is just about fifty miles from anywhere in all directions. Not to indicate its loneliness, but to point out an Arizona fact of life. Once you venture fifty miles from Phoenix, you are now in a sort of no-man's-land, still owned by the Indians and partially possessed by the Mexicans. The whites who have been raised there are aged by the severe sun and wind, adding thirty years to their appearance. The newcomers are the regulars at the dermatologists after the first year. Speed is another realm that defines Arizona; speed is calibrated by time from place to place. I suppose it was a carryover from the Old West, when speed was a measure of how many days' ride it was to your destination. Urban beltways around Phoenix generally get police attention when the speeds exceed 80 mph. Two-lane roads, like Route 93 to Las Vegas, are generally limited by the curves or slower traffic. Then there are the mountain roads. These are the challenging obstacles to travel... hairpin turns, curving on unguarded cliff sides and crazy drivers. It was October 21, 2005 that I spotted Eighty abandoned on the lower part of Route 89 south of Yarnell. I spotted him in the late evening lying at the berm of the highway, partly hidden by the grass. I thought he was a coyote tugging something off the road. It was a quick glance, so I couldn't identify him as a dog. Saturday passed without further thought about the sighting. Then Sunday morning, I decided to run my motorcycle up Yarnell Hill—just past the Frog and Sandy's diner. I saw him—now in bright sunlight.  It was a dog—in the same location and curled up at the edge of the highway. Those of you who travel this road know it is a speedway with heavy traffic. I turned the bike around and slowly approached the dog. He got up and ran back into the weeds and cactus. Then I discovered the reason for his persistent vigilance. Lying deeper in the thicket was a larger dog that had died from being hit by a vehicle. It looked to be a mother dog, and this must be her pup, Eighty. I had a great concern that the pup would find a similar fate, if not rescued soon. I didn't try to approach the dog since the bike had spooked him. I went back home, got the Jeep, some food, water, and a leash. I had made a reference to his location by noting the road sign at that spot...Route 89 and I thought if I caught him, I was going to call him Eighty-nine. After several attempts to leash him, I decided to gain his confidence and sit down and coax him to get some food. My first attempt failed, so I decided to rest the issue a while and go back later on Sunday and try again. I did, and with greater success. I even had him taking bits of food from my hand. I tried to grab him only to miss in the attempt. I decided that a different approach might work the next morning, Monday, the twenty-fourth. I took my van and parked it along the roadway near the dead dog, but Eighty wasn't in his usual spot—he had dragged an old pair of jeans I had put down for his bed over nearer to the dead mother. Again, I started the coaxing with bits of hamburger—this time he followed me at a much closer distance. I concluded that he may have been waiting for a vehicle to pick him up, so I opened the van door and tossed a few bits of burger up to the door and

a few inside—in he went. Now, as I drove away, he couldn't get close enough
to me, whereas only a few hours before, he wouldn't get close enough to catch.
He is a very smart seven month old pup with a real loving personality. I
noticed a natural instinct for him to heel. He survived five days and nights
alone in one of Arizona's most treacherous areas, full of snakes, predators,
cars, and trucks. Well, it's now over a month since we adopted Eight. We have shortened his name to just plain Eight. He is a charmer; one could not find a better companion. I only hope that I live long enough to give him the care he deserves. The crisis I anticipated when introducing him to Rufus lasted only a few minutes; then while directing Eight as to what's what in the dog kingdom,  I noticed a pleasant expression on Rufus's face. Now, I must say that I have special powers of analyzing dog language, both body and sound, and they were enjoying their new relationship. During the course of the new month, we had a few spats and chirps. It is still not certain who was doing the chirping. Today I went back to the site where I found Eight. I was amazed to find the fur and bony carcass of his mother. She was slightly stockier in size and a few shades darker in color but shared the same head and indiscriminate placement of hair and fur- even in death, the resemblance was remarkable. I told Eight a few moments ago, I hoped his mother's soul could

sense his present home and how well he is doing. I still can't believe that Eight escaped the fate of his mother. The traffic on Route 89 is heavy and fast. Coyotes are routinely slaughtered as they go across. But five days in the wilderness and my accidentally seeing him—was no coincidence, I been set up. Well, Christmas came a little early for me this year. My friend Hank made Eight a nameplate for his collar. Hank wanted a dog, but there is another dog for him. I hope that Hank takes the bait the first time when he has the chance for a new companion. It's my life's experience that when opportunity knocks, "open the door." I'm so glad I did with Rufus and Eight. Their presence in my home is as important as the air I breathe. He is almost a perfect dog. He walks with me, and he talks with me. I'm going to have to move him now.

He's under my chair, and it's time for our dinner. There's a special relationship of man and dog reflected by our use of words like dog and God. Is it the combination of letters or a reflection of the truth?

Horatio senior prom…

Horatio, my nickname for one of Wally's friends, walked up to me at Harry's
Pizza shop. "Dave, see that building over next to the furniture store?" "You
mean Black's warehouse," "You got it". Horatio's trite reply. So trite,

we began to refer to him as, "You got it, Becker"
behind his back. "I'm going
to own that place soon." That was a big idea
from the original Horatio Alger
clone of the era. Becker, Wally, and Becker's
sister were hangers-on. They
would pop up at the Baylor's Drive-In about nine
thirty every evening. Becker
was addicted to old Buicks. He liked the 1939
sedans. These were the days
when sedate senior citizens purchased Buicks,
taking great care that they
might last forever, only to trade them off every
five years for the next great
Buick. Somewhere in Becker's mind-set, he
recognized the value of those
well-cared-for old Buicks. They would have
lasted forever had it not been
for Becker's bad vision, bad driving, or a
combination of inept factors that
destroyed Buick after Buick, one after the other,
by driving them into bridges,
rolling over in fields, or clipping parked trucks.
Becker, himself played with
fate like he played with Buicks.

About a month later, I questioned Becker about
that warehouse; "Where are
you going to get the money to buy that
warehouse?" I never got an answer
that my intellect could follow. Later at every
encounter, I would pose the

same question, never receiving a qualifying
answer. The rub here was that
Becker and his crowd drifted off into the sunset
in another old Buick, —I
suppose, popping up at some other diner and
spurting the same unrealistic,
unfunded dreams to anyone who would listen.
The irony of this is that some
thirty years later, I would acquire that Black
warehouse for my own business.
I recall Becker's conversation while keeping our
pizza warm on the hood
of his old Buick. Little did I realize I would be the
one to grow and prosper. After
Becker drifted away, his dreams went with him.
Years later, I did catch a glimpse of Becker still
working a failed scammed system that would
eventually defeat him. I focused on his nicotine-
stained fingers, a ghost of a little boy laying in
his casket. The day of his funeral, I spoke to his
son and was surprised
by his professing the same vision of himself that
bedeviled his father. It follows that ones future
resembles building a brick house. Brick houses
are not erected simultaneously but brick by brick.
Life's rewards are realized the same way.

I enlisted in ROTC at Penn State in a special
(finish college enlistment program sponsored by
the US Air Force) - It was concluded at induction
that I failed the medical. I was reclassified 4-F.
The Air Force released me into to a new void.

I was dealt a devastating blow to my self-esteem, but a relief to my parents.
It was many years later that I considered my lack of military experience again.
I missed the major wars, in any event—I might have been involved in the last of the Korean conflict. Right or wrong, it's the human interaction that fascinates me about being involved in a consuming state of conflict. I felt cheated either by the Air Force or my own perspective that I never served my country in war, but I reminded myself, and others like me, that we have a responsibility to our country in other ways.

We have chance meetings as we go through life. I met this man, now deceased, in Wickenburg, Arizona. He and I had a brief five-minute discussion about war—he impressed me. His story was life altering and mentally stretching. His appearance was not necessarily appealing, but his eye contact caused me to
address him while we were standing in line at a common grocery store. What
was it about him that caught my attention? I do not know—it is a mystery to
me how I make these chance encounters, but I do. I have always attributed
it to God's influence over me. I would like to speak more about this subject
right now, but it can wait for a few more pages. We walked outside in the 105-degree searing noon time heat with a  bright sun burning down

on us.  He remarked about it as he pointed to a small but noisy airplane roaring overhead. He said, "Are you going out to the air show tomorrow?" I don't recall my answer, but I did go that next day, It's what he told me during this brief encounter that was so moving.  John Pinney said he was born in Canada, learned to fly in the 1930's and joined the British Air Corps at the beginning of the Second World War. He caused my patriotism to melt into my lack of military service to hide in a shadow of guilt. I can only relate this experience to those brave ones that touched me personally.  John Pinney, a hero to the world at age 19, flew a P-38 fighter in service to our country protecting the heavy bombers that pounded Europe back to its senses.  Twelve graduates of our eighth-grade school lost their lives in the conflict and the few who returned to lament lost limbs and damaged souls from the experience.  Milt who served as a navigator on a B-24 Liberator survived twenty-seven bombing missions over Germany and lived to tell about it. He trained in the waters near Cuba on a twin engine B-25 in preparation of Jimmy Doolittle's bombing mission over Japan. Milt remarked that these were unforgiving planes and most of them were lost in training exercises. I can't resist covering some of these elements of my background since they weighed so heavily on my mind as a youngster.

I was considered, Mr. Lucky, by my small circle of friends. My dad worked at

the movie theaters running the film machines. I could go with him and see
the films for free. The newsreel showed the war reports, week after week...
death, destruction, misery, and sadness. War solidifies the ingredients in a deadly soil compost guaranteeing a new more grievous future conflict. Life's obstacles contribute to the fulfillment of life's patterns. The Second World War was finally over—things normalized the five years of conflict in about five short months. Society stepped into a great breakaway of daring without concern for failure or harm—a wonderful time of expansion and resolve, finishing the twentieth century with a bang. That bang came with the destruction of the Twin Towers at the hands of a new-organized threat to everything meaningful. There is a random factor in the universe, choice. It eliminates all other possibilities. I have always maintained that as a species we interact and counter act... that's what you do in a herd or a flock. I observed natures' struggling at Park's duck pond. The issues of struggle keep us strong, perhaps Darwin understood this, innately or intuitively. Look at the little wars unrecorded in history, the conflicts of individuals. It is not surprising to assume that war is a natural condition. It is fostered by those who oppose war more than those who embrace war. I mentioned before, war and its consequences have been relevant in shaping my view of the world. Can we dismiss the middle "C" meltdown in Shakespeare's

account of Julius Caesar? It was the short knife that ended his life, not a handgun. "We come to bury Caesar, not to praise him." If good men do as William wrote it, good will be interred with their bones. This is a pointed example of exercising "choice." As we move through the centuries, we see that man has searched for a better life, the freedom to eliminate all other possibilities. That explains why men will conquer the oceans, strike out across the lands, and eventually will reach into a realm beyond this earth.

Cycle middle "C" meltdown...

Perhaps my fascination with two wheels is a result of my stock car meltdown. I remember vividly, several years before the warm-up experience, going to a picnic at a small amusement park adjacent to the stock car track. I was immediately taken by the greasy, dusty motorcycles with the soiled saddlebags and leather fringes hanging from the handlebars. I had to be pulled away from them as they gathered for a Gypsy Tour event sponsored by the American Motorcycle Association. I was about twelve years old and could see myself riding into or out of the sunset on such a bike. They were dirty, but underneath the veneer of dust and mud, I could see the real value of those pinstriped fenders, the neat little lights, and those big Indian heads and decorations on the gas tanks.

The leather appointments were carefully studded with shiny brass and
chrome doodads and buckles. The seats were big enough to support a pony
or two people. I have always been keen on looking below the dust of people's
personalities for the substance of their humanity. I have been amazed by
what I found; it truly made me a believer in not to judge a book by its cover.
My mother and dad were spreading our picnic lunch as I inspected every
element of those leather-clad people with boots laced from the toe to the
knees and pants that reminded me of the animal trainers from the circus. It
was a midsummer day and we offered one of the riders a seat at the picnic
table. He had traveled from Harrisburg, about 150 miles, to join the event. He
seemed to be a cowboy of sorts in his dress and mannerisms, like a character
right out of the Roy Rogers movies. His steed was a Harley 61 knucklehead,
as he called it. My dad, although not interested in motorcycles in particular,
liked everything mechanical and electrical. Our new friend had some potato
salad and a dried beef sandwich with us while telling us about his ride earlier

that morning just before daybreak when his
lights failed. This immediately
spun my dad's intervention into the motorcycle's
electrical world. I can't
remember the rider's name, only how he looked
in that lion trainer's outfit and
a sort of sea captain's hat with a spread eagle
right in the center. I'll call
him, Cap.  He drifted away from our picnic table
to join the other riders.  Cap
returned and asked for some of the coffee from
our thermos bottle; then it
started. Dad said, "I'll take a look at your bike
and see if I can repair your
lights." Cap joined my dad in the project as I
wandered around the campsite,
which would be the overnight quarters of the
riders. They were putting up little
tents and starting small campfires. The beer
truck arrived about one o'clock
and began to give away mugs of beer. My
mother pulled me away from the
crowd as often as she could; she didn't want me
to see them get rowdy, which
they did.  It was rowdy for a twelve year old, but
those people were having a
great time. Over near the racetrack, they were
engaged in some strange racing
events such as slow racing, riding a greased
plank, riding under a string of
hot dogs taking a bite as you piloted your
motorcycle over the wet grass. Cap was running
around the group telling everyone how crafty my

dad was for fixing his lights. They were about to hoist Dad onto their shoulders and carry him like a conquering hero when the roar of the racers caught everyone's attention. That was really something, all those bikes sliding around a circle and stirring up dust and the smells of burning oil. "What a wonderful day," I said to myself. "Someday I will be doing that," and as the years passed, I did, and I still do.

"There's a fellow on the phone for Dad—it's Chris Elliot." Dad spoke on the phone for a few minutes, came back to the basement, and told Bear about the fellow on the motorcycle we met a few years ago at the amusement park. Chris turned out to be Cap; he was coming to the house that evening for supper. I was speculating about his arrival. I visualized his motorcycle, perhaps a new motorcycle with a sidecar. I could still remember his boots that laced up the front from the toe to the knee and the dusty saddlebags that draped over the sides of the knucklehead. I just sat on the back steps looking and listening for a graceful two-wheeled steed to come up the road. Just before supper, a stake body '46 Ford truck rumbled into the drive—it was Cap, I mean Chris. No leather boots, no animal trainer pants, but perched on his head was the same winged eagle cap that stated firmly he was a motorcycle man. Dad and Chris shook hands. Chris put his arm around my shoulders and said, "You have really grown up." He was right, at least partially correct because my driver's test was coming up that March. I suppose the reason for the truck Chris was driving was the remaining winter cold. There were still a few patches of snow around our hills, so motorcycles were not the best choice for travel. Dad said, "Where are you living?" Chris described the location. Dad immediately recognized it, and so did I—it was only about five miles away. I said, "Man, that's great. How about a motorcycle ride?" It was as if I had wished so intently that my future came true. Chris explained to Dad that he and his brother were going to open a motorcycle shop right here in our town, and he wanted my dad to help get their shop ready with wiring and electrical work. During supper, my mind was caught up in the conversation and the plans for the new shop. I didn't actually sleep that night; I only envisioned how I might fit the picture. A week later, Dad began working evenings on the shop preparation, and new motorcycles started to arrive in nice wooden crates. The crates in themselves were works of art. The motorcycle names were classically painted on the sides with neat-looking images of riders having fun. Chris and his brother were busy putting them together and painting the outside of the building. I overheard Chris ask my dad to wait for some of the money for the work he was doing, and my dad was always agreeable to wait to be paid for his work. It was important to get the shop ready for the spring buying season, which was already on us. I felt like a real partner there; it was almost a bloodless family operation.

The weather was now getting warmer, and I passed my driving test. I had to
pinch myself—what could be better than driving up to the motorcycle shop,
piloting my dad's old telephone truck and getting on my very own motorcycle.
The dreamy part was, "my very own motorcycle."
Yes, I was driving now
and Dad's work was nearly finished at the shop. Just being around those
beautiful black-and-red trimmed bikes, breathing the smell of oil and gasoline,
leather—fantastic. I felt more at home there than my own bedroom. I became
aware that wanting and getting expensive nonessentials like a motorcycle
required work. That was my plan—work, get money, and buy a motorcycle. I
was now a little more than just a gofer for dad. I was sawing BX cable, wrapping
wires with friction tape, and even soldering wires with an alcohol torch.

Accidents can change your future…

A new family moved in two houses away. There were three girls, all older than me. One day by accident a fellow by the name of Bear stop at our house by accident, a mistake that lasted for several life times, looking for one of the new girls. After my Dad pointed Bear in the right direction, their conversation went on to a new level. My Dad had been holding a piece of electronic gear that interested Bear…that interest continued well after Bear and our neighbor were married. Bear became a fixture at our house, stopping to see Dad before seeing Jan next door. "Davy, go and tell Jan I'm down here." Jan would wait around, talking to Mother till Bear and my dad got bored with whatever they were doing.

That's when I cultivated my secret interest in watches. Bear's family was in the jewelry business. Bear had samples and watches to show and sell everywhere he went. I had an opinion that working on little bits and pieces would somehow compromise my manhood. So for nearly fifty years, I suppressed my interest by hiding my tinkering with watches. This would later consume my total being as watches became my avocation and my hobby. Bear was my mentor, just as my Dad was Chris's and many others that came to our house. Bear continued to visit our house, and as he was getting more interested in Jan,. He was also getting more interested in money. He was working on the side selling watches and jewelry for his father, who had a jewelry store in a nearby town. As time went on, I became hopelessly mechanical. I was fascinated with machines. It began when I was a toddler. As soon as I would receive a toy car, I would remove the tires. Mother had to hide screwdrivers so that I couldn't dismantle the house. This was not a bad thing since I began to focus on the watches Bear was trying to sell. I got a small set of screwdrivers from Bear and some old watches to take apart. That next summer, my experience landed me a job in the jewelry store of Bear's father. I did everything from sweeping, cleaning windows and display cases, and eventually putting new straps and bands on customers' watches. I had some windfall capital—from Grandma, Dad, and Mother—that put me behind the wheel of a 1933 Chevy master deluxe sedan. I remember the day we bought it—$250—it was a dream come true. It was big enough to carry my bass violin. It transported me to my music jobs at local VFWs, American Legion's Elk's, Moose, Polish clubs, and Italian clubs. I was playing with the best orchestras around. I had always wondered why I was so popular with the bands as a bass player. It was the result of my ability to play the piano. I could stand behind the piano player and read off his chart or watch his hands. That saved the orchestra leader

money not having to write a bass part or purchase the music. The really good musicians didn't need music scores. They just played, and I could follow the

piano player. This was how I improved as a piano player.

By now, you can see how circumstances wove me together, pushing me along as if I was rudderless. That wasn't all bad as I found myself becoming a jack-of-all trades, in the mold of my father, with a sort of a Farmer's Almanac approach to life. Farmers who lived around our community also worked in other industries, like mining, railroad, manufacturing, and building—a way of life that broadened your capacity to survive. Most had been bitten by the Great Depression and were able to endure its hardships. Born in the midst of this social disaster, I was fashioned by it as well. The Second World War followed, and perhaps because of the war, the financial depression gave way to a political depression.

Chris was not doing well with the new motorcycle shop, and I would stop and gloat over the bikes trying to figure a way to get one. Up until now my experience with motorbikes was limited to my neighbor across the road. He had purchased a Whizzer-powered Schwinn bicycle—Dr. Drass was a very busy doctor who made house calls. He had purchased the small farm and began to fill it up with children. I suppose he had visions of his seven year old someday riding the Whizzer, but my curiosity with the bike and interest in it gave way to Doc allowing me to ride it around his fifteen acres.

I rode the Whizzer summer and winter, repairing and replacing the belt
drive monthly. I managed to put over two thousand miles on it, as indicated
on the bike's speedometer, over the years. It really wetted my appetite for
a real motorcycle. I tried to help out at the motorcycle shop, hoping I
would build up some goodwill money toward a motorcycle. I can recall the
day as if the powers in heaven opened their motorcycle door to me. Chris
was confiding to Dad that he needed more time to pay for all the wiring.

On the way home, I asked Dad about his talk with Chris. "David, Chris
is just getting started. Pennsylvania has only a short warm climate to sell
motorcycles, and he asked me if I could wait till next spring to get paid."

My busy little mind began to spin a solution to Dad and Chris's dilemma.

"Could he pay you with that old Hummer bike in his shop?" Dad didn't
say a word about the subject for about a month. It was October, and Dad
figured that the cold weather would dampen my interest in the bike. I saw
Chris about a week after my talk with Dad and started to work the deal

from the other side. "Chris, would you consider trading that old Hummer
for part payment of Dad's electrical bill?" Now I had set the trap to span
both sides of the path. I'm not sure how it worked out in dollars and cents,
but by Thanksgiving, I was riding the Hummer all over town. The Hummer
was a curious little bike. It required a cup of motor oil to be mixed with each gallon of gasoline. On a windy day, if you were riding with the wind, the smoke from the exhaust would follow you or engulf you in a blue cloud. This probably was the origin of the phrase, "Some bikes are so slow they can't get out of its own smoke." I was having the time of my life. Much later in life, I realized that my special skills were in communication and salesmanship. Need being the mother of invention. I went about bartering and trading things all through high school.
The summer before my senior year, I was playing in a band with Bill Alwine.
He was telling me that his brother, who ran a small bakery, needed a salesman
on a route near my home. I jumped at the chance, and they had a real neat
1951 Dodge panel truck. Bill worked in the bakery loading trucks—he set
me up with bread, pies, cakes, and donuts, and I would take them around the
route and sell them door-to-door. What a great job. I got an order book and

a list of customers who were already buying pastries but owed the previous
driver about $200. I had to sell and collect the outstanding debt at the same
time. Well, times were tough in 1953. The war wasn't even ten years old and
certainly not forgotten. There lingered a depression of spirit, a bitterness, that
Americans lived with, having had sand thrown into their grease—I believe that
the pastries lifted many a spirit as well as adding to the weight of the ladies on
my route. This was when I learned how effective sampling the customer was.
I liked cherry pies the best, so I would carve up one of the pies making about
20 samples to tempt the ladies—if they didn't take the samples, I could finish
the pie myself, although that never happened. On a good day, I would carve
up as many as three pies for samples. Monday was one of my busy days. That
was washday, and by 10:00 AM, the ladies were ready for a snack. I cleaned
up the back debts by adding 25 percent to each new order to be applied to
the outstanding balance. It worked great—within a few weeks, I had everyone
current. I quit my bakery route about a week before my senior year.

Those were my formative years. The rest of my life is a tangent to these events

along with many more I haven't recorded here. Each decade created a new
stepping-stone to the next. Marriage came early in my third decade, as it
did with my first two daughters, five career changes, three houses, a college
degree, and my launch into independence with three small businesses. It
was my blastoff, an impatient vision of the future that I considered the most
character building of all my sports. Those that acquire this discipline will
succeed; those who are impatient will thrash about in the water attempting
to create waves, only to attract sharks. My misfortune was that I didn't know
about this rule, but I was fortunate to practice impatience on dry land. There
is one species of shark that has evolved with legs, arms, and the ability to
survive outside the oceans. That third decade of my life was like a Midwest tornado. I really
stirred up the dust and thrashed about. I have always had a vision of being independent and
self-employed. The third decade, which began in 1966, was my initiation decade.
While still employed as a pharmaceutical detail man, I started a motorcycle business in my
garage. A lesson still unlearned was "Those who do not learn from history are destined to repeat
it," and so I did. I should have seen the struggle Chris had with his bike shop, trying to make
enough money in the five warm months to carry

him through the miserable winters here in Appalachia. But I was different. I would change all that, wouldn't I? My day job suffered and I decided to devote full time to selling the new small bikes from Japan. That was the X factor that changed my course from that of Chris. These new bikes were inexpensive and door openers for those without the money for a big bike. Sales were strong. It looked like you could make enough during the warm weather to carry you through the winter. It worked for two years until the competition grew, and the novelty wore thin. I was hired by Yamaha in their eastern office to help build the company. I was later moved to Los Angeles but the strain on me and my family to relocate put an end to that relationship. The changes taking place in the industry and the growth put a premium on motorcycle industry people—I went to work for Skokie Steel in Chicago, who represented Kawasaki. Early on, my commissions were spectacular—things went well for me and Skokie; however, Kawasaki saw the profits all going to Skokie and its sales force and cancelled their contract—effectively forcing me to work directly for Kawasaki for much less money and under restrictive company rules. I returned to manage my

own shop and look at the automotive business. I
have forgotten the identity
of a mythological figure, who with snakes in her
hair, took off simultaneously
in all directions—but that was my third decade
business model.


Independence really only exists in one's
imagination.  Society has created an
interdependency process that tests your designs
with intellectual grit.  Group think analysis throws
sand into the grease of imaginative young
inventors.  Armed with assumptions as to why
something won't work is considered more
important by academics and bankers, than why
something will work.  What might have been
accomplished if it had not been for the isolation
of revolutionary ideas in science by non-scientific
minds?  My Chemistry Prof. commented that
unless you are creating a profit or a miracle
everyday for your employer your job is in
jeopardy.  He suggested that as soon as you are
hired after college, go to work for a big
company… look around for what they are
throwing away… then figure out a way to sell it.
That thought lingered long into my ambitious
personality.  I can point to several instances
where I put the suggestion into practice.  I
always sought to be the upper middle man – the
man who gets the best price, gets the "one-up"
on the competition… never paying the fools
price.  It only took me a few minimally profitable

encounters to see that the light at the end of the tunnel was to be the manufacturer of products and not the lowly distributor.

It was near the end of my motorcycle distribution agreement with Velocette in England that I saw the need to control my destiny and not be compromised by the failure of others.  I believed that I had made a great move – becoming the exclusive distributor of the famous Velocette motorcycle.  Little did I know that Velocette was in trouble with England's labor party demanding many costly factory improvements that would spell the end of my motorcycle distribution company.   The realization that you are unwittingly entangled with others, whether you chose to like it or not is an ego negative.   The impasse between labor and Velocette resulted in the factory closing forever.  My wonderful opportunity lasted only two years and collapsed because of reasons beyond my control.  I commiserated my losses and stepped forward planning a closer look into the ultimate point of control… become a manufacturer.

As the final season for selling Velocette was approaching I looked for an opportunity to engage the growing motorcycle market.  I confided in a friend of mine that I believed that you could sell anything if the product was presented in a clever manner.  We were traveling to a motorcycle industry show when the subject came up – off the top of my head I said,

"How about special oil for motorcycle chain?"
My friend said that wouldn't sell because people
were in the habit of simply squirting a little oil out
the "time honored" oil can. I bet him that by the
next year on the way to the industry show I
would prove him wrong. I did. It was a real
challenge to get over his comment. I could see
that the "time honored" stuff had been rapidly
changing for the better. Better clothing, better
fuel, and better everything to make racers go
faster and ordinary riders demanded it. The first
challenge was to create the right product.
Motorcycle chain has special needs, it must
penetrate the rollers, be lasting and not soil the
rider. Years earlier the major motorcycle
manufacturers all had a small cans of oil labeled
for chain… the riders recognized that it was
nothing special just inflated in price. It didn't sell
and deemed an aftermarket scam. I turned to
my graduate school fluid mechanics course for
inspiration. Putting a solid carbon (graphite) and
a binder into oil seems to be an answer,
producing a special product, carbon black,
making my special chain oil look different.
Motorcycle chain was assembled in friction links
without miniature ball bearing. I considered
adding granulated brass to the black oil to
provide the ball bearings I conceived would
enhance the chain oil. I had now assembled a
formula ready for testing. With the offer of free
oil to the motorcycle racing crowd the monitored
results proved this was a winner. Now the
dispensing… we were now in the age of plastics

so I chose a flask like container that could be easily handled forcing a pressurized stream of oil on the chain. The concept was taking shape in my mind and it was time to locate the oil, the graphite, the binder and brass granules… Robert Burns enters the concept again… "The best laid plans of mice and men are subject to adjustment". Wow, the cost put a halt to the entire idea. It seems that economics sneaks from its hiding place every time it comes to making a profit. I went over the project collecting quotes, asking for special prices on all the ingredients and failing to approach a profitable balance sheet. Giving a plan time to rest gives the innovation gremlins a chance to think about the issues. One of them suggested that I contact an oil re-refiner. Re-refined oil is less than half as expensive as new oil that might be the answer. Considering the cost I decided to look at the re-refined oil producers, there happened to be one in a nearby town. As luck would have it, the refiner, Mr. Wentz, was going to close because the market for re-refined oil had been shrinking. The market was shrinking because better economic conditions work against frugality. I later got a call from the refiner asking what I needed the oil for. I forgot about my rule of keeping my counsel close to my vest and told him about the intended use. He invited me back for a talk. "Dave, There are four railroad tank cars out there full of used oil. Now, when that stuff lies around for a year or so the solids go to the bottom and I think you could just use the oil like it is". His generosity stayed with me for a few days so I decided to open the door of opportunity again. Recalling my Dad's comment about the white wall tires I put it aside as not being applicable in my oil adventure. I did some research on the used oil. This stuff was drained from the crankcases and gear boxes of literally thousands of vehicles over the past ten to twenty years. I measured the contents of four tanks estimating that there was about 35,000 gallons of used oil – it didn't take long for me to see the potential profit in this if I sold 8 oz for $1 and used the entire 35,000 gallons... that would leave me with ½ a million dollars after packaging costs.

A week or so went by and the free oil just wouldn't let me sleep – night after night I would wake with a new twist to consume those 35,000 gallons of used oil. My chemistry background and experience with changing oil in my cars further light my oil fire. I went to the local high school and inquired about using one of their microscopes. It was willingly given to me for a weekend loan – much to my surprise, as I looked through a 60 power eyepiece at a few drops of oil I had just drained from my car, there were small particles of brass and other soft metals in a kind of suspension in the used oil. There was also a sediment of black stuff (carbon) – a by product of combustion.

"I'll take it"! I said to Mr. Wentz on the phone early the next day. I didn't know exactly how I was going to market this stuff but I new this would be a home run with the bases loaded. I started inquiring about small plastic bottles finding that this was going to be the easy part. Now getting it from the 10,000 gallon tank cars then into 8 oz bottles was another issue. Certainly, I thought, remembering railroad tank cars running through town on their way to be broken down into some useful size… I didn't research it much; I simply went to an industrial supply catalog and purchased a hand cranked liquid transfer pump $82. Now that I could pump the tankers I had to find used 55 gallon barrels and a small pump to transfer the oil to the 8 oz bottles. That went easy – I would drive my Dodge truck down to the tankers with two 55 gallon barrels in the back, fill them up – take them back to my motorcycle shop and create the "new" chain oil. Having not been in the business of mixing chemicals or acting like a manufacturer, I had to come up with a new business name, and a name for the chain oil. It is truly an inspirational exercise naming new products and creating a company identity… names range from the ridiculous to the sublime – the laughter this exercise creates will linger in your memory forever. I decided "Penn Chem Industries" would carry the banner.

I suppose my opinion of university education should be revised somewhat, since I was applying something I had learned from my chemistry professor – find something that's being thrown away and figure out how to sell it. The formula was working in reverse. It could be considered bottom up rather than top down. Fogginess was lingering in the back of my mind – ethics, taking something that was free and making a profit… since my chemistry professor endorsed this ideal I regained my senses and went right to work on finding a suitable name for this stuff. I recall the amusing laughter in picking the company name, only to sit here smiling about the beer drinking afternoon we settled on the name, "Old Reliable Chain Oil" with the preposterous slogan "Used for Years" printed right on the label. We continue to chuckle to this day about the truth in advertising policies in the world of marketing; or, the concept of, the truth and nothing but the truth.

Well, that's not the rest of the story, it was only the beginning… marketing started by attending the international motorcycle show in 1968 in Daytona Florida. With the labels having been printed the day before leaving for the show, we loaded twenty gallons of Old Reliable, 250 plastic bottles a small transfer pump and a funnel into the race van. We were part of the early multi-task generation. I was also showing the Velocette motorcycles - seeking sales from dealers and consumers. The 20 hour driving time to Florida found me in the back of the van swaying back and forth trying not to spill the oil while filling the bottles. It was still winter in the northeast but the smell of the warm sea air in

Georgia came through lifting me into an enterprising state of mind. During the fast paces events in Daytona I nearly lost sight of why I was there… to sell Velocette motorcycles and chain oil.

Speed week in Florida was a compressing social, business and vacation event kicking off the coming motorcycle season. Having endured all the social and business potential I could pack into those six days we left for home with a few orders for new motorcycles and a curious notion that we didn't make any progress selling chain oil. I gave away the 250 samples to visitors at the show and assumed that was the end of the hype on the chain oil business. Nearly a month went by and I received an inquiry to buy more chain oil. Then a few phone calls came in saying the flask like oil container was just right for carrying the oil to the races. I found that those who got the samples were dirt track racers and riders. Motocross was just hitting the American turf. Motocross had been very popular in Europe but just like soccer it was now becoming the rage in the states. One of the motorcycle magazines that featured my motorcycles also saw the importance of catering to the new motocross riders… The editor asked me to show him around one of our local tracks, one in which I personally helped to layout. I got a great plug from the magazine as the editor wrote a story about the chain oil… now it was a hot new item.

The editorialized publicity really puts the light on "Products – like, Old Reliable". I began to place small ads in the motorcycle magazines and offer samples to racer and riders. The response was better than I anticipated, since the editorial component of advertising is the real meat… we had an "Old Reliable" tee shirt that sold better than the oil. With the catchy phrase on the back, "Oil Your Chain" and the slogan, "Used for Years" on the front – I began to see the 35,000 gallons of used oil turning into gold. One of the problems with any new industry faces is working capital and credit. Those who saw the potential in starting a new business were traditionally dreamers and not considered real business men – especially when it came to borrowing money to fund their new businesses. Basically they ran on a COD basis. These new entrepreneurs were accustomed to paying for every delivery in cash. I decided to force the market. I visited my local library's Yellow Page section and tore out the motorcycle dealer listing for about 10 states where motorcycling was popular. We packaged 24 flasks of chain oil to a case and put a reorder card in the box, then sent a few hundred cases out COD. They all bought and got a free tee shirt on the reorder…best of all, this was one product they made more on than they paid for it. The dealers loved the profit and the riders liked the Old Reliable. I soon learned that Mr. Wentz was selling out his entire business, land buildings and all. That included my stock of chain oil.   I was offered 60 days to get the 34,000 gallons out of the tanks, but after that, he would have to dispose of it before the new owners took over.  I made a quick sale of Penn Chem Industries to a car dealer friend who also sold motorcycles – I got a new Oldsmobile and a promise of a nickel a bottle for each bottle of oil they sold.  Well, the Oldsmobile was all I ever got.


Meanwhile:

As the production of Old Reliable continued I began to see the strength of our nations economic growth… take a natural resource – refine it to an end product – sell it to some other nation – take the income and separate it to cover cost of conversion, the balance to be divided between reserve savings and dividends. Today, we are on the verge of losing this valuable formula of prosperity.

Back to basics…

 I had been earning the money to fund the chain oil business from my own auto and motorcycle dealership.  This is another story.  As I mentioned my multi-tasking personality had me operating my motorcycle business, bottling chain oil and later a performance synthetic motor oil called PC-2.  I put the earnings from working for Kawasaki as a dealer development person into opening a Datsun (now known as Nissan) dealership. Not content with just the Datsun brand I added SAAB automobiles to the list. Let's go back to the timing of these events. Remember this was less than 10 years since the end of World War II and the Korean conflict and we now entering into the Viet Nam mess – America, especially residents of Western Pennsylvania were still angry about the loses in the Pacific in both blood and money. Cars and motorcycles from Orient were considered traitor haulers.   The only reason they gained a foothold in the US was price – a low price that was funded by the federal government through the Marshall Plan. It was a hidden tax – an incentive to rebuild Japan at a cost to the US tax payers. There was a new problem developing for me on a local basis. The reason I got the financing to purchase 20 automobiles at a time was simple…banks made their money borrowing money from the federal reserve a 2 % interest – lending it to me at 7% interest then placing me in the retail position of selling the cars to the public at about 12% interest…. all transactions flowing through the bank along with a very nice profit. The banks really controlled everything. To add insult to this clever situation, loan officers positioned themselves into the mix of things acting as document processors for the state auto registration laws. How sweet is this?  In my business I decided to have my wife become the document processor for my business, cutting out the local bank loan officer.   This was a costly move on my part, why?  The loan officer got even by making the retail loan requirements nearly impossible for any customer ready to purchase one of my cars on credit – it left me with selling fewer cars, and new pressure from the bank wholesale division to give them more retail sales or they would reconsider funding my auto purchases.   I felt my independence melting away and dissolved the automotive side of my business.  Later I learned that there were more devious plans to take over my auto franchises and put them into hands that were in lock step with the bank.  This was one of my bigger lessons, one that was a blessing in disguise.  I learned that unless you are basically dishonest you are at a disadvantage in the automobile business.

College was not highly regarded, certainly the materials in literature, history and mechanics were interesting, but only to the end that I would be informed. Throughout my life, I considered higher education a place of information—not a ticket to a higher income or status. Men are not judged exclusively by academic achievement or dollars in the bank—but by their kindness. Samuel Coleridge's famous poem, "The Rhyme of the Ancient Mariner," depicts a sea voyage with tragic yet redeeming value, paraphrased as follows: The Ancient Marinere, the character from the poem by Samuel Taylor Coleridge, 1798, relates his tale aboard a ship that sets sail into the  South  Atlantic Ocean somewhere north of the Equator (the Line)—perhaps Florida. The journey takes the ship south along the Atlantic Coast of South America, around the cold and turbulent waters of Cape Horn, then north into the Pacific Ocean. Superstition engulfs the voyage; while in the rough, dangerous, and depressing Antarctic seas off the Cape, an albatross began to follow the ship. Some of the crew hailed the bird as a good omen; others deemed the bird responsible for the treacherous weather. One of the crew, the Mariner, killed the albatross with a crossbow. The fog and nasty seas were blamed upon the bird, and therefore, as the ship continues into the Pacific fair winds and optimism engulfed the crew again, they agreed that it was good for the albatross to die. As the ship continued upon the northward course with fair weather, the Line was crossed again. Suddenly, the ship was becalmed . . . the sea was still . . . the sun did burn . . . "Water, water, everywhere and not a drop to drink." The crew placed the shame, misfortune, and dead bird around the Mariner's neck in an act disavowing the superstition they embraced. One by one the crew all fell to the sea, leaving only the Mariner to contemplate the journey. The calm was finally broken. The angels sent the Mariner alone again. Eventually the illusionary and solitary Mariner reached land. He is compelled to tell his story to relieve his pain and shame to all he encounters with this message, "Be kind to all...beast, bird and man alike." My mother always appreciated great literature. In her last years, she asked me if I had the Coleridge poem. She told me to review it again for its meaning. Mother was leading me to use the message to better the world. That was the basis for her son's life.

Postlogue:

*I'm thinking about taking a walk along the path to the river it's not far from home, its rippling baptizes those who listen closely. Now an exercise that revives my spirit by suppressing the events required for survival. I'll slip into my walking shoes, grab my trusty walking stick and venture into my future. Walking has always brought a sense of meaning to my life. Moving along I remark to myself how congenial the path, although bumpy and muddy, it seems to be in concert with the blades of grass holding it together; not in contempt, but simply cradling its direction. As I focus over the fence I can see the boundary of my life just as the grass nurtures the path. Without any warning my two big friends romped over the pasture and penetrated the boundary that separates man and beast. Their friendship is genuine. They're always interested in my thoughts and asking me if today they would be riding with me or simply opening the gate to their favorite pasture. In seconds their events of the day are interacting with mine. It seems that boredom to them is being stalled on a sunny afternoon. Boredom to me was not that easily defined. The concert between the grass and the path is the model of God's work in nature. The discourse to God's plan for man has become a painful pitch ringing in my ear. There's a place to rest near the river. If you ever walk that way, an unseen attraction invites you to rest and sit awhile. The ringing is suppressed by the ripples in the stream. It's easy to judge the equation of nature by dividing the chaos of life by the ripples of the stream. Peace comes easy here by the river and it stays with you all the way home.*

Made in the USA
Middletown, DE
10 December 2021